WHAT IS IN YOUR HAND?

A Journey Toward SHALOM

SARA L. COLLISON
AND
LEAH M. WENDT

ISBN 978-1-64458-638-9 (paperback)
ISBN 978-1-64458-726-3 (hardcover)
ISBN 978-1-64458-639-6 (digital)

Christian Faith Publishing, Inc.
832 Park Avenue
Meadville, PA 16335
www.christianfaithpublishing.com

Printed in the United States of America

Credits

Photography by Leah M. Wendt, M.A. Adjunct Faculty/Professional & Graduate Studies, Cornerstone University, Grand Rapids, Michigan.

Photography by SHALOM coach Alyssa (Collison) and Matthew Brandt.

B.W. Beckermeyer Photography; Former Studio located at 349 Parchmount, Parchment, Michigan. 1965 All rights reserved. Used with Permission.

Photography and Travelogues by Janet and JD VanderMeer, Encouragement Tours and Events, Division of the MTT Group, Inc., Middlebury, Indiana.

"Memorial Tribute" 2012, used by permission from Dave Person, Freelance Writer for Kalamazoo Gazette.

Foreword and Memorial Tributes by Michael Collison, with Tributes from Holly & Dan Collison from Homestead North.

SHALOM, Inc. Newsletters, by Pastor Keith Lohman, Executive Director of SHALOM, Inc. All rights reserved. Used with permission. 2007–2018.

Dr. Dee Crittenden, "A Celebration of Service in God's Love," SHALOM, Inc. 17th Anniversary, 2007. Booklet used with permission.

"2007 Homestead 20th Anniversary Presentation." Text, letters, and photos used with Permission by Sara Collison.

1995 SHALOM, Inc. "Making a Difference." Originated by Glen and Sara Collison. Lawrence Productions. Funded by Al Dixon/ SHALOM, Inc.

Ryan Smit, Home Manager@SHALOM Three Pines; "My Season of Friendship," 2016.

Zella B. Davis, "Our Wedding Story," August 26, 1965. Anchor Point Camp.

Joshua Pardon, and Marjorie Viveen, *The Poor Farm: A Documentary*, DVD, produced by Joshua Pardon and Marjorie Viveen, (Ottawa County Parks Foundation in association with Ferris State University, Big Rapids, MI, 2017). Special thanks to research from Sara Collison, Julie [Kortz] Stevens, Kurt and Beverly Schroeder, Fred Johnson, Glen Okonosi, Chris Loughrin, Ellen Denny, Meredith Slover, Gerrit Sheers, Jim Budzynski, Wallace and Jane Ewing, Debra Sturtevant, Robert and Janice Mahaney, Linda Vivian, Katie Van Huis, Geoffrey Reynolds, and Craig Powers.

In Memory of Glen Collison (1941–2012), *the gentle shepherd with a vision and the heartbeat of SHALOM*

And with gratitude to our daughter Julie (Kortz) Stevens, who has followed in her father's footsteps with tenacious perseverance, passion, obedience, and vision to continue serving at the first *Homestead* together with her husband, Robert (Doc), and family and with the SHALOM Inc. network.

And with gratitude to Michael and Linda Collison, Dan and Holly Collison, and our precious grandchildren: Alyssa (Matthew), Ryan (Sara), Rachel, Logan, Walker, Atley, Calvin [Kyra], Noah, and Brendan [Taylor]. You are faithfully sharing the *next generation's call* to use what God has placed in your hands.

CONTENTS

ACKNOWLEDGMENT

With deepest gratitude to my dear Goldstein and precious Collison family, for the rich heritage of love and faith. With thanks to my many sisters and brothers in Christ, whose partnership with us in SHALOM brings praise and glory to God.

With thanks to Professor Leah Wendt, the master weaver who took an untold story and made it into a beautiful living tapestry! And thanks to her dear family and to her Aunt Magdalene Waterlander, who believed in this project. What a privilege to accomplish this task together in obedience to the Spirit's call!

And thanks to my granddaughter and SHALOM coach Alyssa (Collison) Brandt for her insightful photography. Also, thanks to my grandson Noah Kortz, the SHALOM Polk Street House Manager and a SHALOM coach.

With thanks to SHALOM Inc. board member, Dr. Dee Crittenden, for sharing her writing and editing expertise. Your red pen was our friend!

With thanks to *our bookends*, Pastor Keith Lohman (Afterword) and Michael Collison (Foreword), for *sandwiching* our story between *two slices* of life.

With thanks to Ryan Smit for sharing your beautiful *season of friendship* with Glen. You are a precious gift to your SHALOM Three Pines House brothers.

Thank you to Harry and Edna Meier, Tom and Shirley Hill, and Al Dixon who believed in our dream and financially supported our vision for SHALOM, Inc. when it was only an idea on a piece of paper!

With thanks to Dave Person for his compassionate articles, which mirror his amazing Christ-centered support for adults with developmental disabilities.

And to Janet and JD VanderMeer, who drive and thrive on long journeys with friends; you obeyed the *Macedonian call.*[1]

And to our first draft readers, Judy Vlietstra and Karen Shorb, whose feedback, powerful prayers, and words of encouragement kept us running the race for Jesus.

And thanks to the anonymous contributors who show God's goodness in providing for SHALOM Inc. To God be the glory, a God of wisdom, love, mercy and grace who has orchestrated the details of my journey toward *shalom* and who recently brought me successfully through breast cancer surgery!

With love to our readers, I pray your journey toward *shalom* will bear much fruit for the Kingdom of God.

With love and gratitude,
Sara Collison

---

[1]   "What is the Macedonian call?" 2018, *GotQuestions,* https://www.gotquestions.org/Macedonian-Call.html

FOREWORD

by Michael Collison
(son of Sara and Glen Collison)

I had decided to be a rock star!

Not for Halloween, but for real. This was a couple of years after beginning guitar lessons and buying my first electric guitar, a thirty-dollar pawn store special. I spray-painted the guitar with leftover chocolate-brown Rust-Oleum. Even though I was only thirteen or fourteen years old, I fixed clearly on "guitar player" as *the* perfect career and my future identity. This dream job fired-up my imagination and fortified me to continue the serious, sore-fingered working of my scales and barre chords, breaking only to hone the intro of "Stairway to Heaven."

Figuring out what you want to be and do when you grow up is difficult because, well, you aren't grown up. And popular youthful career choices are broadly composite, almost cartoonish: archeologist, dancer, musician, actor, teacher, scientist, chef, soldier, athlete, firefighter, detective, writer, police officer, zoologist, astronaut, pilot, veterinarian, and doctor. The plethora of varied real-life jobs and careers that most of us hold is quite specialized, and most lack colorful uniforms, grand work venues, high-tech gadgetry, and cool accessories.

Go ahead and click a program list from a university or technical college, sift through the acronyms from A.A.S and B.S. to W.I.S.E, and you may find it challenging to know what a field career might look like, let alone figure out a dress-up costume. When you weren't grown up, how did you imagine *your* future life work and vocation?

Woven throughout this book is this question: what is in your hand? It was my father's summary of Parker Palmer's two life questions: what am I meant to do? Who am I meant to be?

Parker J. Palmer said, "[There are] moments when it is clear—if I have the eyes to see—that the life I am living is not the same as the life that wants to live in me. In those moments I sometimes catch a glimpse of my true life, a life hidden like the river beneath the ice. And I wonder: What am I meant to do? Who am I meant to be?"[1]

So if I told you that the whole guitar-solo-shredding-to-a-packed-arena thing didn't work out for me, you wouldn't be surprised, right? Failing to join an ascending band didn't prevent me from pursuing a variant career. I went to a private conservatory of music in Chicagoland to become a music major, classical guitar—very legit. Though I had sold my black Les Paul Custom, I worked to salvage a career in music.

As it turns out, I didn't really like sitting in a music studio cell for six hours perfecting Bach Partitas and grinding through even more scales. Meanwhile, volunteering at a local church in a large middle school youth group, I discovered that I really liked teaching kids. This was a place that enlivened me. So I put in my paperwork to become a music education major. Now that definitely had real job potential: a classic vocation—teacher.

But by the time I was handed my music ed. degree, I had fallen so deeply in love with doing youth ministry and pastoral ministry in a church setting, that I veered my vocational trajectory yet again. I tossed my guitar and musical aspirations into the back seat and began an adventurous twenty-five-year run as a youth pastor/pastor, serving the greater community while being on church staff.

Supporting a family of six and a nonprofit career required me getting a master's degree in Moonlighting, Thrift, and Creative Financials. My many divergent side hustles included, but were not limited to, construction day worker, pool table technician, guitar teacher, homeschool band director, substitute teacher, newspaper delivery person, product tester, speaker, writer, and drum builder.

The journey from aspiring guitar hero to vocational pastor was an unimagined career plot twist. However, as I served for a few decades in local faith communities in New York, Michigan, and Wisconsin, focusing on stu-

---

[1] Parker J. Palmer, *Let Your Life Speak: Listening for the Voice of Vocation* (Jossey-Bass: 2000), 11, 15,16-17, 36.

dents, teaching, and community service projects, I felt a deep abiding satisfaction that I was spending my life wisely and well. This is what I was put on the planet to do. I am making a difference. And then, the church cut my position!

Churches, like people, age, lose revenue, and shift focus. So nearing age fifty, I finally had to set aside my pursuit of a dream career. I needed a job. Oh, I tried to find an exciting new venture, frantically applying for dozens of "amazing new career opportunities," but absolutely nothing moved. Grand possibilities vanished, so I signed on to sell frozen food door-to-door.

The company loaned me a truck, inventory, a handheld computer, a uniform, and an established route. Each day, I stepped up into the cab and drove deeper into an extended and disorienting season of vocational tumult. What does one do when one doesn't know what to do? What is next when every possible door remains locked? When our hands are empty? Do something and keep the bills paid to provide for your family? The preacher had to move to the other side of the pulpit.

As I lugged two bulging bags of frozen food from my delivery truck to the door, I thought, *Absolutely nothing in my five years of private, liberal arts college prepared me to be a worker. I was trained to be a leader and change agent, shaping the world, and all I have to offer now is Shrimp Scampi and ice cream—two dollars off.*

My stint as your neighborhood frozen food guy ended when I was recruited by a local specialty foundation repair contractor to put together solutions in people's homes; this was a classic outside sales role. My guitar player, music teacher, youth pastor, pastor-self could never have comprehended this new plot twist, affirming the Proverb: "People make their plans, but God directs their steps." When I grow up, I want to be a System Design Specialist and help people fix their basements!

In God's great mystery, the many loose threads of my earlier life were rewoven together into a new and vibrant workout on the road helping people fix major foundation defects. At the point of my greatest vocational emptiness, a powerful, surprising convergence arose. All that I have been, the teacher/pastor/construction worker/community service leader/outside salesman fused into my current vocation, which allows me to bring all of these to bear on my new daily work. I travel a three-hour service area, meeting people, inspecting their homes, and putting together custom permanent solutions. It turns out that I am really good at this and am able to help both customer and company with renewed vigor and purpose. Imagine that! This was not my plan, but then, my life is not my own.

Leonard Sweet said, "Your life is not your own: it belongs to God. To *be yourself* is to be and do what God wants you to be and do, knowing that God created you for a mission and knows you and your mission better than you do."[2]

I share this brief sketch of *my* journey from Rock Star to Basement Rock Star and my quest to discover my work and calling because the story you are about to enter belongs to my parents. My first half of life, I was intertwined with *their* circuitous path of vocational discovery. I was passenger and partner in a number of their adventures in serving the special needs community and the beginnings of a new nonprofit organization, SHALOM Inc.

Over their decades together, my parents lived many roles: nurse, CPR Trainer, elder care nurse, floriculturist, horticulturist, butcher, grocer, dairy farmer, foster parents, adult foster care managers, nonprofit developers, chief cook, and bottle washer! What emerged was an evolving and complex lifework that managed to gather, borrow, and build on all the previous, that exclaimed, "This is who we were called to be! This is what we were put on this planet to do!"

This is a two-story book. It shares my parents' personal journey of vocational discovery and their search for *shalom* (the Hebrew word for peace) in a spiritual calling, but also the story of the birth and growth of a nonprofit organization that serves adults with developmental disabilities in community. As these stories are shared, there is an invitation for you, the reader, to reflect: *What have you been given to work with? What can you do with it? What is in your hand?*

Ultimately, most of us desire to create a personal legacy—something impactful that will outlive us. There are no shortcuts to this. My parents, like many other people of faith, sought to do so with great intentional consideration toward being faithful managers of all that their Creator had endowed them.

"How do we discover our work and calling?" Henri Nouwen states, "Christian discernment is not the same as decision-making. Reaching a decision can be straightforward: we consider our goals and options;

---

2   Leonard Sweet (2002). *"Soul Salsa: 17 Surprising Steps for Godly Living in the 21ˢᵗ Century", p.11, Harper Collins.*

maybe we list the pros and cons of each possible choice; and then we choose the action that meets our goal most effectively. Discernment, on the other hand, is about listening and responding to that place within us where our deepest desires align with God's desire. As discerning people, we sift through our impulses, motives, and options to discover which ones lead us closer to divine love and compassion for ourselves and other

people and which ones lead us further away."[3]

Likewise, Isaiah once wrote of God's mysterious ways, "You did awesome things that we did not expect."[4]

This book that you hold in *your* hand, tells about one couple's journey toward *shalom*, to use what they possessed for a different but greater good than they had ever planned. In the mystery of it all, my oldest daughter continues to be a coach for SHALOM. Alyssa is loving on the special

needs community, caring for a variety of animals on the same land my father cultivated, while studying communications and nonprofit leadership.

The hope is that, as you take time to read about this journey of a local community ministry, that you too will catch the story within the story—the spiritual challenges within the pages.

---

[3] Henri Nouwen, *Discernment: Reading the Signs of Daily Life* (HarperOne: 2013), 17.

[4] Isaiah 64:3 NIV.

As you pause to consider *what is in your hand*, may you be stirred to action. The people in your life and neighborhood need you to discover "where your deep gladness meets the world's need," and live into it.[5]

With gratitude,
Michael Collison
May 31, 2018

---

[5] Frederick Buechner, *Wishful Thinking: A Seeker's ABC* (HarperSanFrancisco: 1993), 119.

"Leah, just come over for coffee."

By the time we had finished writing this book in 2018, Sara Collison had nicknamed me The Weaver. At first, I did not know a *heddle* from a *treadle*. Glen was a weaver and a spinner! So Sara taught me about the *warp and weft*, also called *warp and woof* in the King James English Bible.[1] To *weave* this book, Sara first handed me *the warp*—pre-strung threads held stationary on the loom—booklets, DVDs, CD rom, a zip drive, newspaper clippings, photo albums, scrapbooks, travelogues, newsletter articles, personal letters, Facebook postings, thank you notes, prayer journal notes, awards, and even a powerpoint with Glen in it! All these items were *pre-strung* for me. Next, Sara provided me with *the weft: strands* from a lifetime of stories, names, faces, and dates. Since I knew little of SHALOM Inc.'s backdrop, my *basic pattern* for *weaving* the story became a travelogue style of journal writing.

---

[1] Leviticus 13:47-48, KJV.

The idea for a book—*The Loom*—was set up in late July 2017. My husband, Roy, and I were out shopping when we met Sara Collison! We told her about our granddaughter's joy over attending the 2017 Farm Camp@SHALOM, which hosted Bible stories, nature lessons, farm animal chores, fun activities, camp crafts, garden chores, and hayrides for elementary-age children!

I said, "Your SHALOM farm is really amazing, from sheep to alpaca! Your residents were so helpful and kind to the kids and filled with enthusiasm. Has anyone ever written a book about how you started this nonprofit organization?"

Sara confessed that writing a book was something she felt God wanted her to do especially since Glen's sudden death in 2012. So I offered to help her write down some of these memories. However, I soon began to feel very overwhelmed by the sheer volume of stories *woven* into a *forty-three -year tapestry* of ministering to people with developmental disabilities. Where do we begin?

Sara simply said, "Leah, just come over for coffee!"

I did. Then in a step of faith, I looked at that *giant loom*, prayed for *patterns*, and picked up *the shuttle* (ePEN) with a single story *thread* in my hand!

Edith Schaeffer explains the process in her book *The Tapestry:*

> Each of our lives is a thread. You are a thread, and I am a thread. As we affect each other's lives, physical beings, spiritual understandings, or material possessions, or as we influence each other's

attitudes—creativity, courage, determination to keep on, moods, priorities, understanding, spirituality, intellectually, emotionally—we are at the same time affecting history. History is different because you have lived, and because I have lived. We have each caused ripples that will never end, and we continue to cause ripples. In the picture brought to our minds by *The Tapestry* (and our book too) we are being woven together, threads that are important to a pattern, the pattern of history of our lifetimes, but also the pattern we affect in the future in history.[2]

Thank you for joining us on our journey toward *shalom*.

Leah Maria Wendt

---

[2] Edith Schaeffer, *The Tapestry: The Life and Times of Francis and Edith Schaeffer* (Waco, Texas: Word Books, 1981), 14–15.

Sitting in Sara's Glory Room

6191 North Riverview Drive, Kalamazoo, Michigan
September 14, 2017

A s I drove around the circle drive to Sara Collison's home, I was greeted by stately trees backlit by the morning sunlight. From a peaceful vantage point near a white gazebo, I could hear the musical sounds of farm life. Not everyone has alpaca and sheep grazing near their front yard!

Upon seeing Sara's home, a two-story barn makeover, it was hard to imagine that chickens once lived in this building. Next door to her home stands the pioneer home known now as The Homestead, renovated to become a licensed foster care home for twelve adults with developmental disabilities. Glen and Sara had purchased this condemned nineteenth century Michigan farmhouse in the spring of 1987 and acquired the farm property a few years later. After six months of major renovating, The Homestead was dedicated to service on October 12, 1987 by Pastor Roy Ackermann of Haven Church of Kalamazoo, Michigan.

I glanced over to the stately old house (The Homestead) with its wraparound porch and thought about all the work that Glen and Sara and their family had put into that project to make it a home for twelve adult residents. Surely this was where the story of SHALOM, Inc. all began. I was soon to learn that just as God had prepared King David as a shepherd in a sheepfold first, so God had raised up Glen and Sara with years of preparation (1965 to 1987).

I was about to find out more about their ministry story since Sara had invited me over for coffee to talk about her dream of writing down these memories, "Memories of an extraordinary God of *Shalom* (peace)."[1]

As I entered the hallway of the lower story garage with adjoining office space, I passed by a wall displaying very old photos. If the cliché is true that *a picture speaks a thousand words*, a whole book full of stories was staring at me. Looking at one photo and reading the tiny print, I saw that Sara had won a 1993 Secretary's Award for Excellence in Nursing. Someone had also once told me that Glen had milked cows and won awards too. I can't wait to hear about those stories. Since I am a pianist, the old player piano with a stack of music rolls also caught my eye. I would soon learn that Glen played piano while Sara played the organ. I thought Glen only played accordion, and Sara only played violin—what a surprise!

I knocked at Sara's door and was greeted by her but was also greeted by another surprise going up the stairway to her home on the second floor. The stairwell and the walls were decorated with hand-hewn wood siding to look like a real log cabin! What a creative trick. I was indeed immersed in a *log cabin on the inside* not visible from the outside. I would never have guessed that. From my first impression, I drove up to

---

[1] Thomas Simcox, "The Other Names of God," *Israel My Glory: A Ministry of the Friends of Israel Gospel Ministry, Inc.* 61, no. 4 (June 2003): 17–18.

a modern vinyl-sided home on a farm. Maybe this is how the Collisons came to know adults with developmental disabilities: the creativity hidden inside awaits to surprise us, to delight us, or to change our views!

Walking up the stairway, I viewed the huge American flag, old but dignified, claiming a prominent spot in the stairwell. At the top of the stairs, I saw another musical instrument, an old pump organ. Sara said proudly, "And here is the picture of my Jewish mother, Dorotha Goldstein playing the organ."

I loved the photo of the old log cabin church (Zion Evangelical Lutheran in Northern Germany Township, Wadena County, Minnesota). I soon heard about how the organ had come to the Collisons' home. I realized that every inch of this creative home was laden with stories as rich as this one. I saw the Hanukkah candles and a shofar horn and really wanted to hear more stories from her Jewish heritage. Would she be surprised to learn that my father's family was Syrian?

Well, I was excited to see that Sara had set the table with coffee and homemade baked chocolate chip peanut butter cookies (a real treat for me since I love them but do not make these at home due to a granddaughter with peanut allergies). Karen, a SHALOM resident, bakes and sells these treats: Karen's Wonderful Cookies.

A fire was going in the massive stone fireplace. Red pine logs graced the walls and the high ceiling was covered with tongue and groove sassafras which revealed Glen's amazing creativity. Yes, they designed all this.

Sara explained how Glen had worked very hard to prep all these red pine logs and sassafras boards: selecting them, cleaning them, and coating them. She described how such logs have to sit for a year before the bark can be easily removed. Then the logs get debarked with a drawknife.

Her story suddenly reminded me of the scene from the book *Little House on the Prairie* where Pa and Mr. Edwards take the horses and wagon to the creek bottom to haul out the seasoned logs to make the log sill (foundation) for their log cabin. Pa and Ma, plus a neighbor, had built their own home with great perseverance and strength of mind and heart.[2] I was about to learn that those same strong pioneer qualities had set the groundwork for this nonprofit foundation SHALOM Inc.

---

[2] Ingalls Wilder, Laura. *Little House on the Prairie* (New York: Scholastic Inc, 1935), 56.

As we stood in the living room, I noticed the thick steel beam with split red pine logs wrapped over it. Although decorated so uniquely, this major steel beam has the invaluable purpose of bearing the load of the structure. There it was all alone, in the center of the room, strong and silent yet beautiful with a most important twenty-four-hour task.

That center beam reminded me of Glen and Sara: calm and graceful, composed, yet standing up strong as steel under the pressure and the load of daily shepherding adults with developmental disabilities. Others would later follow in their footsteps and work in homes as caregivers to the residents.

While this monumental task might overwhelm so many of us, Glen and Sara and their family, and many staff and volunteers, have stood peacefully in the middle of this ministry, all these years, firm and unmoved, just like the steel beam holding up this high ceiling. Something else, however, helped them bear a load.

As I looked around the room, I saw what it was. Scripture verses are everywhere. This indeed was the Log Sill (foundation) of all their strength. They did not rely on their own strength to remain solid like a steel post in the center holding everything up! The verse on the table stood out to me and explained the bedrock source of their real strength. Psalm 62:1–2. "Truly my soul silently *waits* for God; From Him *comes* my salvation. He only *is* my rock and my salvation; *He is* my defense; I shall not be greatly moved."

This was their Main Beam in the center of all their living. I could see the photos of Glen placed around the room reminding me of their journey toward SHALOM together. Glen died suddenly in 2012, yet the God of *Shalom* [peace] is still the ministry's base. God is also Sara's rock and refuge which gives her stability and a future hope. She misses Glen daily, but joy is evident in her life.

Next, I was invited to see her sunroom which matches the main home space, having a matching red pine log inlay design around the top border. The three walls boast rows of windows, which truly let the glory shine in. Here it all comes together as Sara described the journey to create this sunroom.

She explained, "You see, I realized how dark my living space was with fewer windows and no north or west exposure or outdoor space on my second-floor home. A builder friend, Mike Smith, designed a beautiful addition with a covered outdoor porch. Not wanting to start this project without God's blessing, I earnestly prayed for wisdom.

Answering, God put this idea in my mind, *Call it the Glory Room.* The addition was started May 6, 2015 and completed that fall."

With all this sunshine, I could see why she would call it that, but she meant something deeper. The focal point of the room had a sign with a scripture verse on it. "Whatsoever you do, do all to the glory of God." Sara smiled but acknowledged, "Now this was quite an idea we had to use a red pine log inlay border like this around the whole top of the room to tie both rooms together. Since we built the other half so long ago, we were not sure if we could get similar logs to match. Well now, this was God weaving together the smallest details. Glen's brother Al hosts a woodworker's guild. One of the members who attended the guild meetings knew the neighbor who had provided the original logs for Glen. So my friend Dee Crittenden and I went over there to the Delton area to see him, and we picked up our logs from off his pile. Yes, they were the same kind of red pine logs, just like the ones Glen cleaned and prepped nineteen years earlier! Before we left, he asked us if we needed a drawknife. How amazing. Yes, we would need that. We did not think about where to get one, but God knew we would need one and provided it.

"Then my brother-in-law Al came over and taught us how to use the drawknife. Dee and I just started slogging away and working hard. Then Pastor Keith Lohman dropped by and offered us his curved drawknife, and we soon learned why you really needed both knives to debark the logs. This process was slow, steady, time-consuming work, much like building a nonprofit organization like SHALOM Inc. God had sent the drawknife, then he sent someone to teach me to use it, then he sent the strength, help, and the time to go with the tools. This is just the point. God knows what you need even before you ask for it. He is *Jehovah Jireh*, our Provider. This literally means the Lord "will see to it."[3]

I could see what she meant. SHALOM was built just like this, as a matter of supply with God's talented people in a network of community by God's provision. I am starting to get the picture of why she calls her sunroom "the Glory Room." The whole scene illuminated God's story for His Glory.

The morning sun was beaming into the large open space and was spotlighting a photo of Glen and Sara together.

She noted, "Yes, glancing back now over the years, you can see how the whole plan fits together like one giant puzzle."

---

[3] Simcox, 17–18.

I had to agree that I enjoyed hearing about the creative journey which put her in touch with the original miller of logs after all those years. The inlay border looked great, and the sun porch really did add light to the whole house. The main living area does have large skylights, but the snow from our cold Michigan winters dampens that source. I can see how one might feel like an early pioneer in a log cabin, with one side of the room commanding the giant stone fireplace, and the opposite wall having all the windows.

Glen would be so happy to see their original hard work now supplemented with an enclosed addition of the porch. More than just bringing in light, Sara's new room speaks to her heart with great purpose about design and eternity.

She asked me, "Why do you think we often miss seeing these connections of God's Master Builder plan for our lives?"

Her question is so important. What clouds our *spiritual skylights* to dampen our vision? Sara went on to tell the story:

"We must think of God like a Daddy [*Abba* in Hebrew] who loves to give gifts, big or small, and see us squeal with delight! He wants to give us the desires of our hearts once we give our hearts solely to His Will.

"I have to tell you about how we got the sink when Glen and I built this original cabin side of our home. You see our daughter Julie had a blue porcelain-looking sink. I wanted one like that too. At the time, we went to Builder's Square in Kalamazoo and found the model, but we were told that this sink was only a special-order item and not available for months.

"Glen tried to console me that we had an old steel sink and could make do with that. Well, I tried settling in on the second option but then went on a clearance hunt with what I call my *searching heart.* Lo and behold! There it was, our sink, the exact sink I wanted and on clearance too. Leah, God always sends us what we need at a price we can afford."

Someone else had special-ordered it then decided that they did not want it! Sara and Glen were so thrilled to find what they needed in such good timing. Sara recognized that the sink is a constant reminder of God's delight in sending us his best gifts, just like a father delights to see his children clap their hands and dance with joy over a choice gift! Hers is a personal God, not a distant Creator.

"Why do you think we miss so many moments like this?" Sara asked me.

We were standing in the sun porch room, the "Glory Room" where this message of eternal hope seemed so strong. Sara admitted that she was sitting here meditating one day on our need to drink deeply and slow down and commune with God in his Word. She told me, "I was meditating about this idea of *drinking deeply* after reading a Bible study. I was watching the hummingbirds on the veranda. What a commotion! They were bumping all around each other, flapping madly, all trying to get one little drink. After the mass of little birds flew away, one sole hummingbird returned. It just came quietly by itself to the feeder and drank and drank and drank. Then it flew at the screen door and just stood there looking at me through the screen as if to say *pay attention!* At that moment, I was thinking again on what it meant to do what this little bird just did, drink deeply. We flap around so much in our rush to get what we need. We just need to be still and drink in the word, and stand still and drink, drink long, and drink slowly, all by ourselves.

"This was so beautiful to see the illustration in nature. This is what Glen saw in farm life; simple things on the farm teach us such complex lessons in life. We often waste energy in our hustle and bustle to get what we think we need, but we just need to slow down and listen to God. God can really use creation to teach us spiritual thoughts like this and speak to us. Isaiah 12:3 teaches, 'With joy you will drink deeply from the fountain of salvation!'[4] And the Orthodox Jewish Bible says, 'Therefore with sasson shall ye draw mayim out of the wells of *Yeshuah* [Salvation].'"[5]

Sara's new space has brought more room for meditation. I could see why Glen thought that a working farm and a home ministry to adults with developmental disabilities would be such a marvelous combination. There in the "Glory Room," you could look over the

4   *Holy Bible*, New Living Translation, copyright © 1996, 2004, 2015 by Tyndale House Foundation. Used by permission of Tyndale House Publishers, Inc., Carol Stream, Illinois 60188. All rights reserved.

5   Orthodox Jewish Bible (OJB) Copyright © 2002, 2003, 2008, 2010, 2011 by Artists for Israel International

veranda porch and see those lessons illustrated below: goats, sheep, alpaca, rabbits, chickens, ducks, grapevines, maple trees harvested for syrup, fruit trees, and a vegetable garden!

Looking off the veranda deck, Sara told me, "Leah, I have such a strong memory of this one young man [autistic spectrum disorder] who came to visit the farm. At the time, he was living at home, and a job coach was bringing him to encourage him to work on the farm. While other residents were happily doing morning chores, this young man was off in a corner, alone, arms wrapped around his body. He obviously did not want to join the group. His job coach began encouraging him to begin little tasks. Step by step, over time, he was building trust and interest. More than that, the animals offered him in return unconditional love: he also sensed that they were dependent on his help for food and daily care. The transformation began. Today, he joyfully lives more independently in a supported living SHALOM home, near the farm, sharing life with his house brothers. He is interacting in community, living in wholeness, growing into his fullest potential in Christ. He shows leadership in animal care, while sharing those lessons with others."

As Sara and I walked outside to view the farm after our morning coffee time in the cabin, Sara poured into my heart some last-minute personal encouragement. For eleven years, my husband Roy and I have been after-school and summer caregivers for our autistic granddaughter while our daughter works as a nurse. Sara seemed so well-equipped as a nurse to understand the medical issues that swirl like a hurricane around these precious children with special needs. Yet she has witnessed the care of a compassionate Heavenly Father, who sent the Savior of the Universe to reach everyone. My heart came away cheerful to think a community like SHALOM could offer them a future with hope.

Our morning together made me think of a C.S. Lewis quote, "Hope is one of the Theological virtues. This means that a continual looking forward to the eternal world is not (as some modern people think) a form of escapism or wishful thinking, but one of the things a Christian is meant to do. It does not mean that we are to leave the present world as it is. If you read history you will find that the Christians who did most for the present world were just those who thought most of the next. Aim at Heaven and you will get earth thrown in. Aim at earth, and you will get neither."[6]

---

[6] Clive Staples Lewis, *Mere Christianity* (New York: Harper Collins, 1953), 134.

Before I left that morning, Sara had quizzed me and challenged me on one more thing. "Leah, do you imagine that God is romantic? Oh, you have to hear about our wedding story." Frankly, I can't wait to hear more about this!

Chapter 1 Challenge: God's name is *El Olam.* This is Hebrew for Everlasting God, the God without Limits, hidden, concealed; time immemorial, time past, antiquity; eternity, without end Genesis 21:33.[7] Find your own special quiet place, your Glory Room. Andrew Murray offers us this challenge, "O let the place of secret prayer become to me the most beloved spot on earth."[8]

---

[7] Simcox, 17-18.

[8] Andrew Murray, "Prayer Resources," *Prayer Coach,* May 18, 2011, sponsored by Josiah's Covenant, all rights reserved, https://prayer-coach.com/prayer-resources/

A Wedding Story!

Today, while driving to the farm, I heard a quote on the radio show *BreakPoint* by Eric Metaxas, "The Lord can use imperfect clay pots like us to accomplish great—no, in this case *astounding*—things in this sin-scarred world, if we're willing to make available to Him all that we have."[1]

When we hear about an *astounding* married couple in this "sin-scarred world,"[2] we may become more curious about their story. Some might say that they were just the lucky ones who just happened to find Paradise in each other's eyes. Was Karma or Fate just guiding them? Did they just deserve each other or by chance find that *True Love's Kiss* like a Disney character in a film?

After my last visit to Sara's cabin, she had left me with a lingering question, "Leah, do you imagine that God is romantic?"

Well, I have been thinking more about this fresh outlook. Yes, the world needs a clearer vision of an infinite unfailing love out there matchmaking.

As I drove up to her cabin for our Thursday morning coffee chat, I was weary and recovering from a week of *record-breaking* temperatures in late September. Michiganders are generally used to chilly fall mornings with a little sunshine breaking through, but we are not ready for ninety plus degree temps demanding air conditioners and more Gatorade than fresh-pressed apple cider or donuts!

---

[1] Eric Metaxas, "Go See 'Mully' the Magnificent," *CNS News,* 2018, https://www.cnsnews.com/commentary/eric-metaxas/go-see-mully-magnificent
[2] Ibid., 18.

I was grateful that Sara had a refreshing treat waiting for me. She made her favorite coffee: home ground Berres Brothers Highlander Grogg, with a combination of caramel, butterscotch and hazelnut! Amazing stuff! I did make her chuckle when I asked if the coffee cream in the little cup was goat's milk.

Sara said again how Glen was always experimenting with creating new recipes: he liked using goat's milk and making everything from cheese to ice cream. Once, Glen had given me a quart of this same rich natu-rally homogenized goat's milk to make my Dutch grandma Lena's tapioca recipe! It tasted so different than using store-bought milk; what a rich flavor! I realized how we can get so used to *skim milk* experiences, that we view something normal in God's plan as *record-breaking*! God made us and knows us; he has a plan for marriage.

While savoring her morning brew, Sara unveiled their wedding album. Looking at the black and white photos, I saw an *astounding* plan that was quickly put into place for the special day of August 26, 1965, exactly one year after they met on August 26, 1964! After hearing this story and how it all unfolded, you may agree with Sara that God wants to send miracles into our everyday life.

Sara (Goldstein) graduated in 1962 from Portage Central High School in Portage, Michigan. Her next step was to attend Bronson Methodist School of Nursing in Kalamazoo, Michigan. By the summer of 1964, Glen Collison had earned an Associate Business degree from Ferris State University (FSU) in Big Rapids, Michigan but was now going to Michigan State University (MSU) in Lansing, Michigan. Sara was still at Bronson, a three-year Nursing School, so their pathways would be literally quite far apart. Sara notes that God was about to test her obedience to wait in faith!

Sara loved the fellowship of the vibrant college-age Christian friends. Going to a church downtown was convenient for nurses liv-ing in the dorm next to Bronson Hospital. They could easily walk past the peaceful Bronson Park to conveniently find Bethel Baptist Church.

However, for Sara, finding her Christian faith was neither easy nor convenient, but the Savior gave Sara peace: the Hebrew word for that is *shalom.*

According to Strong's Exhaustive Concordance, *shalom* means "completeness, soundness, welfare, peace." It is translated "success" and used as part of an inspired blessing from 1 Chronicles 12:18. *Shalom* is applicable to an external peace between two entities—such as individuals or nations—and to an internal sense of peace within the individual.[3]

At the age of sixteen, a next-door neighbor had invited Sara to Bethel Baptist where she had heard the gospel of Christ's love and death on the cross for our sins. She walked down the aisle to pray one Sunday and publicly surrendered her life to Jesus Christ, her true Messiah. Imagine telling your Conservative Jewish parents that you have given your heart to Jesus as the true Messiah. Her father had walked in the traditions of Judaism, but her mother had converted to Judaism.

Sara heard her Jewish father respond in firm tones, "We forbid you to go to another church outside of our synagogue, and you must never share this faith in public with anyone."

Sara had grown up in a loving family, so this put a great strain on their close family. Jewish missionaries supported by Bethel Baptist Church (Vernon and Faith Shannon) later counseled with her to be obedient to her parents. Sara decided that she could still worship the Messiah yet stay respectfully under her parents' roof and pray for her family. For two years, she worshipped *underground* reading her Bible and listening to the radio.

Then in January of 1963, as a freshman living in the nurse's dorm (Bronson Methodist Hospital School of Nursing), she obeyed the Lord in baptism.

She noted clearly, "I was no longer *under* my parents' roof."

---

[3] "What is the meaning of the word Shalom?" *Got Questions*, https://www. gotquestions.org/Shalom-meaning.html (accessed November 13, 2017).

Sara conceded that she had chosen the Methodist-founded school of nursing with the hope of hearing more about the Bible and meeting more Christians. The God of unfailing love was drawing her to Himself in a most unique way.

The news of her baptism brought a heartbreaking response, however, from Sara's father, Isadore Goldstein. In his words, "You are no longer my daughter. You may not come home again."

How did her mom take all this? Sara noted peacefully, "My mom continued to send me care packages to the dorm room, but my father always pleaded with me [via phone calls] to leave this newfound faith. I think he thought it would just die because he had forbidden it."

She did not change. The hearts of her parents and her own heart, however, were about to be changed in the most *astounding* and unexpected way. This love story begins with a sudden crossing of paths and a case of mistaken identity.

It was 1964, and a friend who had already graduated from nursing school, Joyce Mansberger, had taken a job as camp nurse at Anchor Point Camp near Three Rivers, Michigan. Sara was interested in seeing what a camp nurse might do, so she came from Wednesday evening to Saturday. Sara wanted to learn what a camp nurse needs to know. Sara fondly remembers:

"I was at camp, Wednesday night, [August 26, 1964] out at the ball diamond, when I decided to walk all the way back to the dining hall. Suddenly, a convertible full of campers drove by, stopping to offer me a ride. At first, I turned down the offer, really looking forward to the long walk. However, the driver was offering quite persistently, and I thought I recognized him as Al Collison who attended Bethel Baptist Church, so I accepted the ride.

Sara realized that the tall, young man driving the car, who came around to open the car door for her like a real gentleman, was not Al Collison. Surprised, she heard, "Hello, I am Glen Collison."

Sara was not aware that Al had a brother. Little did she also know that the camp was searching for a handyman that week. Glen had heard about this urgent need at Anchor Point when he was in Sunday worship at Bethel Baptist Church in Kalamazoo (where his grandparents had been founding members). He ended up serving as a high school boy's counselor but could only work from Monday to Thursday since he had to be back in Lansing. What did that really mean for this brief first meeting as their pathways suddenly crossed? Sara responded with a joyful expression, "The Lord literally caused our paths to meet for the first time on Wednesday, August 26, during camp. I thought he was polite and gracious but did not imagine that I would ever see him again. That same Wednesday night, a camper with a sprained ankle had to be driven to the hospital. My friend Joyce [the camp nurse] called upon Glen to drive her since she did not have a car available. I had to stay as camp nurse. After helping Joyce, I did not see him again the rest of the camp week as he had to leave the next morning for MSU!"

The brief chance crossing of their distant pathways might have been the last of their encounters, but God was busy at work. Sara recalls, "I was looking forward to babysitting my nephew Dov while his parents went to the synagogue for the Jewish New Year, Rosh Hashanah [which fell on Labor Day in 1964]. My sister Marilyn from Parchment [in Michigan] had asked me months earlier to babysit for the holiday. I was really very excited to have a break and get out of the nursing dorm and care for my nephew. Amazingly, my sister called me early in the morning and canceled, saying that she did not need me that day as her neighbor was going to babysit, but she would need me the next day instead. Very disappointed, I told my roommate that if I had known I wasn't needed to babysit, I would have tried to get transportation to Gull Lake Bible Conference to hear our Pastor Mark Jackson who was the guest speaker for the weekend. There I was, suddenly free for the day, but with no way to get there. I said in my heart, somewhat sarcastically, *If God wants me to go, He can provide the way!* God really went to work on my heart after that!"

Meanwhile, back at his parents' home in Kalamazoo, Glen had been mulling over whether he should call Sara and take her out. What spot had he chosen for a date? It was that very same place where Sara was longing to go: Gull Lake Bible Conference! Glen had also heard that Pastor Jackson was going to be there. (Glen was home from MSU for the Labor Day holiday.)

He ran the idea past his mom and argued, "Well if Sara says no, that's it. I am done."

Sara laughed, "The phone rang at the dorm, and I was surprised to come to the hall phone and find out that the man I had met briefly on August 26 at Anchor Point was inviting me to go out. Excited, I said *yes.*"

Glen called at 9:00 a.m. and Sara told him that she could not go to the late service on Labor Day because she had to work at the hospital but asked if they could go to the earlier service. Yes! He was there in half an hour, ready to go! She recalls having heard the beautiful hymn during that service: Trust and Obey. The Holy Spirit used every word of that song to touch both of their hearts.

"When we walk with the Lord, in the light of His word, what a glory He sheds on our way. While we do His good will, He abides with us still, and with ALL who will Trust and Obey. But we never can prove, the delights of His love, until ALL on the altar we lay, For the favor He shows and the Love he bestows is for those who will Trust and Obey."[4]

Sara remarked, "It was such an amazing matter of perfect timing that our schedules did match up in spite of the complexities. A week after our first official date in summer 1964, I had to go to the Kalamazoo Regional Psychiatric Hospital for part of my psychiatric training. The Friday following my Labor Day date with Glen, I was walking back to the dorm, feeling overwhelmed. I got back to the dorm, got on my knees and prayed, asking the Lord to fill this strong need to love and be loved or just take it away. After praying, I went back to studying with a restful sense of peace. Very shortly after that, the hall phone rang, and my nursing friends were paging me that Glen Collison was calling. Well, he had done his homework. He would have had to call Bronson School of Nursing and then get a forwarding number to the Psychiatric Hospital where I was in the nurse's dorm!"

On their second date, no surprise that he took her to the Allegan County Fair (in Michigan). He had an insatiable love for agriculture and an appetite to learn all that he could! She also observed that she felt so much peace on their dates. No surprise, she enjoyed a date to another County Fair in Centerville, Michigan. As they dated, she got to know Glen's family. Uniquely enough, Sara suddenly realized that when she was four years old, she had met Glen's grandma Gladys Pike. Neighbors had invited Sara's mom to a Bible study. The teacher with that beautiful flannelgraph was Glen's grandma from Bethel Baptist Church.

Glen came home from MSU whenever he could, but by Thanksgiving, he wanted to meet her parents. Sara felt unsure of her family's response, but Glen gently encouraged her to just make the call. She bravely did. The response was another miracle. While this may seem

---

4   Helen H. Lemmel, "Turn Your Eyes Upon Jesus" (1922).

astounding on one hand, Sara said calmly, "Leah, God is totally trustworthy, but our obedience is vital. God knows what he designed us to do. I love Proverbs 3:5–6, '*Trust* in the LORD with *all* your heart and lean not on your own understanding; in all your ways submit to him, and *he will make your paths straight.*'"

God was also weaving their paths. Glen's father, Lyle, owned a grocery store, (630 N. Burdick Street in Kalamazoo, Michigan) and Sara's father liked that Glen's father bought some of his meat supply from a local Jewish vendor.

By Christmas of 1964, Glen had romantically proposed in front of the nurse's dorm, but they kept their engagement a secret until Glen could afford a ring. Glen wanted to make it public with the ring on her finger!

Next, Sara began praying what she calls "dangerous prayers." She admitted, "I threw out the fleece like Gideon did in the Bible and asked God for solid direction [Judges 6:36–40]. I told the Lord that if He did not want me to marry this man, to stop the engagement ring from coming."

Whenever Glen apologized for not getting the money yet for a ring, Sara only smiled. She meant that *dangerous prayer*. Glen's money kept going to so many other unforeseen college expenses. Meanwhile, Sara kept in touch with her Jewish missionary friends, Vernon and Faith Shannon, who had suggested that she might put in an application for Detroit Bible Institute. No ring had arrived, so she asked the Lord for direction on doing His will and not her own. Is Bible school or marriage the plan? She would need to know by April 5, Monday, in order to submit the application on time to the Detroit Bible Institute.

Finally, by April 3, before Palm Sunday 1965, Glen had a ring, having had an interesting and *astounding* week. He had gotten calls for nonstop work. All the money for a ring suddenly came in the form of extra jobs for one week straight. If the money had not arrived just when it did, along with the ring, she would have submitted her application by

April 5 to go to the Bible College right after graduating from nursing school! This was very *unique timing*: April 3!

When Sara and Glen told her parents, they had an interesting response. The Goldsteins asked Glen and Sara to just go to a Justice of the Peace, go to a Rabbi, or go somewhere out of town, but do not go and have a big church wedding or a public ceremony of any kind. What would they choose?

Chapter 2 Challenge: God's name is *El Shaddai:* Hebrew metaphors are derived from action and not appearance, so *El Shaddai* literally means that God completes the action of satisfying all-sufficiently (Genesis 17:1).[5]

Have you ever trusted Jesus like Glen and Sara were suddenly left to do?

Yeshua Jesus came to earth as God incarnate, *El Shaddai*. He is our Living Water, the Sacrificial Lamb, complete satisfaction.

Billy Graham said, "God is more interested in your future and your relationships than you are."[6]

---

5   Simcox, 17-18.
6   Billy Graham, "Prayer Resources," *Prayer Coach*, May 18, 2011, sponsored by Josiah's Covenant, all rights reserved, https://prayer-coach.com/prayer-resources/

CHAPTER 3

Love United for His Glory

In retrospect, Sara observes that "We can now see the hand of a Loving God with a loving plan, who showed up (August 26, 1965) right in the middle of our hour of need."

The inscription inside Glen's wedding band indeed outlined their story: *Love United for His Glory.*

Sara had planned on being the camp nurse at Anchor Point during that last week of August 1965, even though her family had tried to discourage her from going. Under pressure, she and Glen had even considered just getting married in secret in the pastor's study. That was Plan A, but a second possible option came to light in June 1965.

Glen's floriculture classmates from MSU in Lansing, Michigan, needed a mock couple to come to join in a staged or real wedding so that the students could practice their skills to prepare flowers for a real wedding. Since Sara and Glen were engaged, they were asked if they would be either a *real* couple or a mock couple for this floriculture final MSU exam. The engaged Collisons agreed to the fully paid educational mock wedding adventure in the MSU Stone Chapel.

Students had to work through levels of wedding formality related to the time of day, number of attendants, cake selection, formal versus informal choices, etc. Only Glen's parents were able to come. Wearing an elegant wedding dress from her older sister Rosalind, Sara and Glen had the joy of experiencing a traditional formal mock wedding and elegant reception, all paid for by the floriculture studies at MSU. Why did that not seem to satisfy the wedding dilemma for this young engaged couple?

Sara explains, "The timing was just not right to begin our new life together. We did not sense that this was God's plan for us. I was not going to graduate until July of 1965, and we wanted a Christ-centered service."

By fall, Glen had floriculture studies waiting at MSU, while Sara had a new job waiting at Sparrow Hospital in Lansing, Michigan.

They still had a problem. Sara's mom had purchased a lovely knit wedding suit with the hope that a secret wedding out of town would be their choice. Would a *real public* wedding day be their step of faith?

Sara and Glen faced the challenge to either hide their wedding vows and hide their Christian faith or go public. Sara turned to their Jewish missionary friends again (Vernon and Faith Shannon). She knelt in the home of the Shannons and asked God what to do. Sara was a senior in nursing school, and by fall, she would face many decisions. Glen sought the Lord.

How did it all turn out? Sara handed me a little leather-bound book made from Anchor Point Camp Craft Materials. Here is their public wedding day story from August 26, 1965, in the original words of Zella B Davis and Dorothy Fish:

"One year ago today [August 26, 1964] Glen Collison was working at Anchor Point Camp as handyman, but he couldn't stay all week, just until Thursday. One year ago, Sara Goldstein came to camp to be a counselor, but she couldn't come until Wednesday." Late Wednesday night—they met!

One year later (August 26, 1965)

On this calm afternoon, Sara, Ginger, and Betty talked of a wedding soon to take place and thought how nice it would have been to have been able to get married on the first anniversary of their meeting. The afternoon went on as usual with supper, activity hour, and camp fire. Maxine, Joy, and Mildred stayed away from the camp fire to avoid the mosquitoes and to cook popcorn for the staff gathering after camp fire.

Ring, ring, ring!

An emergency long distance phone call for Sara (Goldstein)!

She was summoned from camp fire. She came running with a panicked look on her face. She called the number and waited. A voice answered. She blushed and giggled and giggled and blushed.

After the brief message, she announced to the kitchen crew that she was getting married that night—that was Glen Collison calling to say that President Johnson had just signed a bill saying all young men not married before midnight tonight were eligible for draft. The time was 8:40 p.m. What to do? Get ready! After the kitchen crew had a good healthy laugh, they nervously started getting the bride ready. Quick, what to wear? It was a choice between a nurse uniform and a (maroon) skirt and (white) blouse. The latter was chosen, and the bride quickly dressed.

The ready bride waited for her groom, who was on his way from Lansing to pick her up and take her to Kalamazoo for the ceremony. He didn't come, and he didn't come, and plans were being changed by the minute, for time was flying. Alas!

At 10 p.m. Glen came flying into the dining hall, accompanied by two of his buddies from school, saying, "Where is she? Where is she?"

Time was of the essence and decisions had to be made and made quickly. Before everyone knew what was what, we heard the car outside start its motor, and everyone ran out with handfuls of popcorn, and began throwing it, but still no one knew quite what arrangements were being made for a wedding.

Glen said they decided to go to Kalamazoo as quickly as possible and be married by Pastor Mark Jackson before midnight. It didn't take much convincing to persuade them to stay at Anchor Point and wait for Pastor Jackson to come up. But if he didn't make it, there were four other ministers of the gospel who could tie the knot. (*That morning at camp coffee hour, Sara had mentioned that this day, one year ago, she had met Glen. Wouldn't it be nice to be married on the exact day? Little did she know that God had a plan for her wedding to include her loving camp friends, in a service of joy, rather than secret vows in Pastor's study.*)

When the decision was made to stay at camp and hold the wedding, things began flying around! People just seemed to automatically fall into a pattern of loving preparation for the big event. Tables were moved to the back of the dining hall, leaving a lovely fireplace setting at the front. One by one things began appearing to set a lovely atmosphere—a pot of greenery from the chapel, wild flowers and firewood (a big stack set afire much too soon but at a time like this, how can one judge just what is going to happen when?)

No candle holders were around, but John Lewis and Zella Davis quickly improvised some with foil-covered bottle tops from the kitchen, and Mrs. DeVries just happened to have four white candles in a box in her room—but things happened so fast when Pastor Jackson arrived that they didn't get lit.

Boys just aren't interested in weddings, so it seemed perfectly natural for two of them to be sitting at one of the rear tables playing a game of checkers. While preparations were falling into place downstairs, God was with Sara every step of the way upstairs.

The missionary's wife (to the Philippines), Jennie DeVries, happened to have a white sheath linen dress with her that had just been cleaned. It was a little snug, but God made sure that seams were wide enough for Joy McAuley's nimble hands to let the dress out. Mrs. DeVries's steam iron made the dress look like new, and she also had a veil hat and real pearls for Sara to wear.

Before dressing, our bride knelt and talked with God. Then with dozens of gals popping in and out of her room, she dressed, and was at once a glowing, beautiful bride. After she was safely dressed, every woman in camp went running here and there to find a skirt or dress to put on, for they at once realized that though the situation was fun, it was also serious.

Downstairs, four long benches were brought in from the chapel and placed in position for the self-invited wedding guests. White hydrangeas were borrowed from mystified neighbors, to be placed at the "pew" ends. The mahogany piano bench replaced the rickety wooden folding chair at the piano. The camper's cabin name cards—Waterbug, Beach Boys, La Mouche, Wipe Outs and Yuckle Chuks—were hastily removed.

Mr. Carlson brought in the mic (microphone) and tape recorder. Mr. Beckermeyer readied his professional cameras—as well as many others with their little cameras. Mrs. Roskam, who has played for so many weddings, took her place at the piano. Mr. Mansberger assumed the part of giving the bride away. And to top it off, the young men who had accompanied Glen to the camp, were also studying horticulture at college, so they went scouting around in the dark for an assortment of flowers and weeds, from which they made one of the most beautiful bridal bouquets ever seen. They were composed of hydrangeas, fern, and Queen Anne's lace, while the groom had a bachelor's button boutonniere.

All this (happened) while campers slept (we think!). Did you ever hear of going out and waking up guests for a wedding? That's what happened, and it was funny to see a few bleary-eyed members of the staff walk into the chapel.

About the same time, something was being done about a place for Glen and Sara to stay on their wedding night. A few starry-eyed girls got the brilliant idea of letting the newlyweds stay in Ruth's maple-wood cabin. All giggles, they ran to the cabin to get it ready, and to look for wedding flowers. They could hardly believe what was happening. Jim Siegle didn't believe it either when the girls pounded on his bedroom window and told him about the midnight wedding.

He said, "What's the gag?"

I guess he started taking them seriously when they started pulling up his flower bushes and taking decorations from his cabin which might be used for a wedding in the camp dining room. At Ruth's cabin, they tried to think of things to do to make the place a cozy little honeymoon cottage. A few practical things done were washing the dishes, sweeping the floor, and fixing up the bedroom. Some extras were putting two coffee cups on the stove (who knows if they were ever used or even noticed), putting a sign on the bedroom which read "Bridle Sweet" (that is the way they spelled it), and a note on their bed which read, "Love is of God."

As a final touch, they started a fire in the fireplace, and turned the lights down low. While doing their busywork, their conversation turned to the terrible situations in the world that had been a main cause of all this night's excitement. They praised God, though, that they could feel secure in his care and guidance. They knew that no matter what happened in this confused world, God had planned everything for His own glory. They were also thrilled at the way God worked out everything for Glen and Sara. It was marvelous, too good to be true, and surely a gift from heaven. By this time, they were all talked out. They realized it was 11:30 p.m. and they had a wedding to go to.

It was still difficult to believe how it all happened, but it was truly marvelous to see how God worked in and through everything and everyone.

Back at the dining room, a look at the clock gave us a jolt because the time was slipping by quickly, and Pastor Jackson hadn't yet arrived (from Kalamazoo to Lincoln Lake). A second look at the clock convinced us that it wasn't even working! It might be later than we thought!

At 11:55 p.m., the headlights of the car were seen, bringing the second most important man of the hour into the campground. Whew! Like magic, everyone was seated (no time for ushers), and a holy hush fell over the room as Pastor Jackson took his place, and the wedding march began. The bride came in dressed in traditional white and glowing with a joy that we feel  most brides miss, after they have done months and months of preparation and are almost too tired to smile. After a solemn and precious wedding ceremony, when the *I dos* were spoken before the stroke of midnight, and the pastor gave them his wonderful words of commitment to the newly established home, Rev. Fred Carlson (who secured the pastor) sang "The Wedding Prayer."

The quick-thinking kitchen crew came out with trays of ice cream sundaes (with whole cherries instead of halves) to celebrate the occasion, and the guests entered into the joyful spirit of a wedding which had been performed.

Before the bridal couple left to go to their cottage, the bride gathered about her all the eligible young ladies and threw her bouquet. Betty VanderBrook never caught one quite as interesting as the one she caught this time.

Thus ended a chapter that began just one year ago today at *Anchor Point* when Glen and Sara first met. How fitting that they should celebrate the date by becoming one in the Lord.

The End! (Written by Zella B. Davis, Anchor Point Camp, August 1965)

Glen and Sara believed that God had brought them together in such a way that to lack faith in His plan would be disobedience. Why did August 26 become so precious to Glen and Sara Collison? More than just a day set in motion by President Johnson's announcement on the radio, the day became a fulfillment of a higher plan, a public Christian wedding day. Surrounded by supportive loving Christian friends, like a family all together at Anchor Point, in that one moment in time, they took their Christian vows and celebrated love united for His glory. (Glen would later complete an army physical in January 1965, only to later have a deferment since Sara was newly expecting.)

Sara expounded on this for me, "God has a plan for each of us. We cannot compare our experiences with the plans designed for someone else. If we do, what will happen? Anger? Frustration? Bitterness? Jealousy? The real crux of the matter is that you will miss out on that perfect plan created just for you."

Isaiah 49:1 (NIRV) explains it this way, "Before I was born, the LORD chose me to serve him. Before I was born, the LORD spoke my name."

Sara's central theme is echoed again by Dr. Peter Marshall, chaplain of the US Senate (1947–1949).

"You are leaving port under sealed orders and in a troubled period. You cannot know whither you are going or what you are to do. But why not take the Pilot on board who knows the nature of your sealed orders from the outset, and who will shape your entire voyage accordingly? He knows the shoals and the sand banks, the rocks and the reefs, He will steer you safely into that celestial harbor where your anchor will be cast for eternity. Let His almighty nail-pierced hands hold the wheel, and you will be safe."[1]

Hearing Glen and Sara's story of how God united them for his glory, I realized that this *record-breaking, astounding* love of God is for everyone.

---

[1] See "The Berean Call," https://www.thebereancall.org/content/under-sealed-orders

Chapter 3 Challenge: God's name is *Jehovah M'Qaddash*, The Lord Who Sets Apart. Do you believe God loves you and has a wonderful plan for your life? The Hebrew "*Qaddash*" means that someone has been pronounced clean. To dedicate, preserve or sanctify implies a precious event, paralleling the Hebrew word for  holy, set apart and precious (Exodus 31). "This name not only implies sanctification, but also that God is the one who cleanses us from sin and sets us apart for His service."[2]

Billy Graham said, "Prayer is not just asking. It is listening for God's orders. Nothing will drive us to our knees quicker than trouble."[3]

---

2 Simcox, 17-18.

3 Billy Graham, "Prayer Resources," *Prayer Coach*, May 18, 2011, sponsored by Josiah's Covenant, all rights reserved, https://prayer-coach.com/prayer-resources/

CHAPTER 4

"I thank God every time
I remember you."

October 5, 2017. The phone rang with an incoming call from Sara Collison. "Hello, Leah. It is Thursday! I know today is our day to work on writing the book about SHALOM, but I can't meet today. I have a file full of photos to sort out for a big presentation this Tuesday at the Shepherd's Barn! We are having a thirtieth anniversary celebration for The Homestead (1987–2017). I have a ton of work to get everything ready!"

Sara had given me a photo album of letters and thank you notes from the twentieth anniversary celebration of the Homestead (2007). After seeing so many photos and thank you notes, I was getting the bigger picture of SHALOM as an extension of our community: donors, volunteers, staff members, residents, board members, house parents, farm helpers, SHALOM Woolery helpers, organizations, churches, college students, trip chaperones, special olympics, and the list goes on, scrolling like movie credits on a big screen event!

Glen and Sara's middle son Daniel, outlines it so well in a letter he wrote for the twentieth anniversary of Homestead event, October 2007.

Dear Mom and Dad, physical distance has a way of implying that we are far apart. This is not true for us. Tonight, as you are honored for your tireless work, we are with you. We have always been with you, sometimes physically, but mostly, in unity of purpose.

Tonight, scores of people will attest to the work of your heart, your hands, your lives. May it be sufficient to say that, if we were there, we would affirm it all and then some. A wise person once articulated that if one wants to find the truth concerning a person, interview those closest to him or her. Isn't it in these relationships where we see the greatest abilities, inclinations, accomplishments and failures?

This letter is our input, and its purpose is to testify to the truth of your lives. Though we often tease Mom about wanting more kisses than Dad has to offer, and tease Dad about having more projects than Mom can tolerate, you are together One Unit. Your loyalty to each other has been the bedrock of your lives together. This wonderful couple who can laugh and cry, love, and defend each other when needed, offers a glimpse of how God considers each of us. It is a security that few people know in this world. You have modeled it beautifully for all to see.

When we married, we were drawn to live near you. And this we did for eight years. Here we learned how to work hard and how to love others, despite the inconvenience it may cause. But most importantly what you modeled for us was the concept that such a small number of people are willing to grasp: You showed up!

Simply that. You were willing to do the work: the hard, stinky, unending, fiscally inadequate, WORK. We know you have cried countless tears wondering where all of the people are. We know that your burden is great, and you have had to rely on supernatural strength to move forward. We know that though you are fallible, you are one of the strongest examples of simple, powerful faith that many have ever seen or will ever see.

All who have known you will affirm that you have touched their lives in countless ways. For us, as your children, we have seen it up close and attest to the truthfulness of this testimony. Your example is now part of the yarn with which we stitch our lives. And when our lives are done, you will be woven into the fabric... our fabric, our children's fabric, our children's children's fabric... We thank you, we honor you, we love you.

Dan, Holly, Walker, and Atley, October 13, 2007

Reading all these thank you notes, seeing the photos of the banquet, and seeing these family letters, really helped me grasp more of the foundational work that went into this nonprofit ministry. To present this same message, Glen had made a presentation for the 2007 anniversary to share what God had done.

He relayed some of the initial goals from 1990. Glen and Sara wanted ministry longevity.

1. Establish a nonprofit organization that would model the Homesteads' Extended Family and Christian values
2. A ministry that would provide continuity, sustainability, and resources beyond what the Collison Family could accomplish
3. Homes that were biblical and Christ-centered and would serve and love those in their care
4. Sustainable care through support to House Parents and Supported Living Coordinator
5. Volunteers are blessed as they see that they make a difference for the SHALOM residents and House Parents
6. Good stewardship of properties and financial resources

Glen presented it this way, "God provided knowledgeable, skilled, and willing people to serve on that first board: Sally Lindsay, Sara Collison, Tom Lowing, Daniel Collison, Noreen Jolliffe, John Westra,

Mark Pulver, and Attorney Garry Walton. Bruce Lenardson came shortly after the first board meeting held October 16, 1990. The three existing Homesteads were to be the model with shared values and goals.

Looking at Sara's scrapbook album, I became curious about more of these celebration stories. I found a red booklet written by Dee Crittenden, "What a special day it was for all the huge Ottawa County Community Haven Family. (a 229-acre dairy farm where Glen and Sara served from 1978–1987, home to 60 adults with developmental disabilities) They piled into the yellow school bus and filled the bus with all the important *stuff* a kid needs to attend college away from home and headed off for Illinois. They pulled up proudly to the curb at the dorm at Wheaton College to launch Mike (Collisons' eldest son) on his college career!"

That same Wheaton College grad Michael shared his heart in a letter which he also wrote in honor of the twentieth anniversary event in October 2007.

Dear Mom and Dad, the transition from the (Ottawa) County Farm to the Homestead (1987) was not an emotionally smooth one for our family. The years, the work, the investment, and the building of nearly ten years, ended bittersweetly. We were grateful for the rich time but saddened by the loss. Though I was busy at college, I felt the weight of losing the home I had lived in and loved during my middle and high school years. At first, Kalamazoo meant little to me. But out of loss and at a crossroad, you began all over. You took every lesson, idea, and experience south to Parchment (Michigan) and poured them into a condemned house.

I have a few hazy memories of demolition and early renovations. Those days seemed surreal to me. But out of the new 2x4s, nails, shingles, plumbing, siding, paint, carpet, and appliances, a new home was created. Unlike the store at Conklin or the apartment at County Haven, the Homestead took time to become my home. With each visit I slowly embraced your new place.

I have no childhood memories in Parchment, but twenty years of meals, conversations, activities, and of course, construction projects fill my mind and heart. (1987–2007)

What is even sweeter to me now is the love of the Homestead my children have. From the sheep shed, to the back porch, to the loft, to the large dining room table, it is the only Collison grandparents' home they have known.

When asked what they love about you and the Homestead, they say things like the animals, baking, the huntin' shack, the Loft, and antiques. They enjoy the fun and friendly spirit that comes from you and the residents.

And for twenty years, a few dozen adults have also called the Homestead their home. This is a gift to my family and the community. Successful living and vocation are highly dependent on fit. You created a home for adults that needed a place to call home. This was good for them, but this was also a good fit for you. Having your own business/home has provided the space and freedom to explore your hobbies and interests while doing adult foster care.

In your quest to build a better group home, you've tried lots of new ideas, some worked, some didn't, but you never quit on the Homestead. I appreciate your desire to offer care that isn't institutional. At the Haven, you worked to make a large facility feel more like a home. In creating the Homestead (and eventually SHALOM, Inc.) you had no barriers to develop a warm and welcoming home for all. The Homestead is a place of work but seldom without laughter and play.

At the (Ottawa) County Farm, there were limits on how your faith could be shared. When you began the Homestead, you committed to make it a Christian home and have cultivated a faith in Christ with the residents over the years. Running any home is a lot of work. ("Hard, stinky, unending work" as his brother Dan noted in another part of his letter.) Every family has to contend with financial needs, personality clashes, repairs, and the day to day chores of life. "The Homestead" is no ordinary home. All of the typical needs of a household are multiplied greatly. It is a big house and a big family.

In addition, you have a home within a home, and a family within a family to care for. This is a complex and challenging daily reality. Over the years, you've had opportunity and reason a plenty to shut it down, but you haven't. I applaud your perseverance. It is an impressive achievement that the Homestead you created and carried for two decades, continues to this day. As you move into the next chapter of your life, may you remember, celebrate, and enjoy all the good that you have done and all the life you have brought to all who set foot on 6191 N. Riverview Drive.

With great Love, Michael, Linda, Alyssa, Ryan, Rachel, and Logan

Their daughter Julie also explains their unique journey together.

Dear Mom and Dad, This day (2007 Anniversary) is a celebration of God's faithfulness in the Collison and Goldstein family. All throughout the family lineages of two very distinct, strong and loving families, one Christian and the other with a Jewish faith, God blended your gifts, your heart and created a family that has been serving others for over 42 years (1965–2007).

From the beginning of your marriage you have been on the front lines of birthing dreams and struggling with some dreams that never came to fruition. Yet, Dad, you press on. (*These dreams like seeds would bear fruit after Glen's death in January of 2012.*)

It is only by the Grace of God and your strong pursuit of making a difference, through Christian love, that your success story continues until today with many wonderful people coming alongside to serve with you.

As your parents passed down a rich heritage of love, faith, hard work and play, it laid the groundwork for 20 years of laughter, tears and priceless memories we have shared within our family at the Homestead with SHALOM. I thank you, and your grandchildren thank you and generations of extended families thank you for your faithfulness and the continual pursuit of showing God's love to all.

Love, Julie (Kortz) Stevens and Calvin, Noah, and Brendan Kortz

Well, on this peaceful October 2017 morning, ten years after these letters were written, I am missing the fresh ground Grogg coffee and Sara's homemade peanut butter cookies. However, after hearing what SHALOM means to everyone, I know her time is being well spent to prepare an anniversary presentation. I can only imagine the difficulty of organizing all the photos and memories to thank all the donors.

There is a wider community goal here too. Sara also wants to teach the next generation about the abundant faithfulness of God. Glen had a similar purpose when he created a huge two-volume family memory album, with notes dating several hundred years back to England. Glen wrote about this challenge in a letter to his family dated August 4, 2010:

To my family: A number of years ago, we heard author Ken Guyer speak at the Gaither Praise Gathering. He was telling the importance of recording family stories with pictures; memories and events are quickly forgotten and the stories make the pictures come alive now and for years to come. This book has been put together with much love and joy. I felt many emotions as I relived, sorted, cut and pasted pictures pulling up memories from the past 69 years of my life (1941-2010).

Many stories came from recalling information told by my folks, grandparents, cousins and Uncle Clarence Altman. Uncle John Pike added much to the Pike section. I want to give a special thank you to cousins Bob Collison, Cathy Collison Ober, and sister Joyce Collison Ross plus other family members who have added pictures and interesting stories.

As this project is nearing completion there is sadness since this has been a seven-year life adventure (2003–2010). I have changed notebooks three times to accommodate the ever-growing unfolding story. I am not saying everything is 100 percent correct (stories from several hundred years back) but there is no one left to verify this! I have tried to make it interesting and informative.

Sharing our heritage and connecting each of us with the past, makes the present and future have a greater impact. As you will see there is a rich spiritual heritage within our families. The faith walk has had a very strong influence. I trust that it will be even stronger in the years to come.

As God is working through our lives, we can see generation after generations that have remained faithful to God's calling. I have tried to add points of interest, humor, and pictures that depict each era. Every generation has had many challenges and blessings. Hopefully, as you travel memory lane with me, you will be encouraged in your life's journey.

I present this to you with much love, Glen E. Collison.

Reading Glen's letter, I could see the heritage that molded this man for ministry. Reading the (2007) thank you letters from their children, I could see just how the Lord had answered all those wedding prayers (from 1965). Next, I wanted to know what events had shaped Sara's heart.

Well, she was twenty-one when she married Glen in 1965. In a few short years, she found out what she called "a new level of responsibility and a better understanding of God's role as a parent to us."

Their first son Michael was born, followed soon by Daniel, then Julie. (Three children born between 1966–1970.) When Sara's father, Isadore Goldstein, passed away in 1986, Glen and Sara made the move to Kalamazoo. Glen noted, "The perfect house was waiting in Cooper Township [the Homestead at 6191 North Riverview Drive in Parchment, Michigan] and became available due to her parents' generosity."

Who or what had changed the hearts of Sara's parents? I could not wait to ask Sara. Was it the same thing that had changed Sara's heart?

Here is the beautiful verse that Julie posted to her parents (Philippians 1:3–6), "I thank God every time I remember you. In all my prayers for all of you, I always pray with joy because of your partnership in the gospel from the first day until now, being confident of this, that he who began a good work in you will carry it on to completion until the day of Christ Jesus."

Most people are used to work—unending, unnoticed, consuming, grueling, and pressing *work*! Few people are used to getting thank you notes for doing the work that even fewer people see! However, God sees it all.

Chapter 4 Challenge: God's name is *El Roi* (The God Who Sees Me). This name for God is only found once in all Scripture. In the Bible, Hagar had run away from her ungrateful mistress Sara. She and her son Ishmael were driven out, alone and in distress. It is there in a state of desertion where she meets the Angel of the Lord. Genesis 16:13: "The God of Seeing."[1]

Take time to write a thank you letter or send a card or start a family memory album to teach the next generation about God's faithfulness!

---

[1] Simcox, 17–18.

"Live in peace *shalom* with each other. Rejoice always, pray continually, give thanks in all circumstances; for this is God's will for you in Christ Jesus" 1 Thessalonians 5: 13, 16–18.

As Graham Cooke has so wisely noticed, "First Thessalonians 5:16–18 puts prayer in the middle of a thanksgiving sandwich."[2]

---

[2] Graham Cooke, Prayer Resources," *Prayer Coach*, May 18, 2011, sponsored by Josiah's Covenant, all rights reserved https://prayer-coach.com/2013/03/07/prayer-quotes-graham-cooke-2/

CHAPTER 5

Powerless and Invisible

I n my last visit to Sara's cabin by the SHALOM Farm, I had asked her about the nursing award hanging on her cabin wall. She pointed out that it came from training staff for emergency situations and came at a unique time in her life when she basically felt like the "invisible nurse" on the evening shift.

It was 1993, at the Battle Creek (Michigan) Veteran's Administration (VA) Hospital, where many patients depended on quality evening care. She worked evenings doing triage in admissions, weekends, and holidays. Glen was the head cook at the Homestead and kept the family going, and he wanted her to keep her nursing skills fresh. Her medical skills also benefited residents at SHALOM. However, her supervisor had recently offered her a difficult challenge. Before moving up to a higher level of responsibility, Sara would have to demonstrate her ability to impact the whole hospital. How could she possibly find time for that, given her limited time at the hospital and her intense involvement with SHALOM.

It was on one of those lunch breaks at the hospital, while she was praying (another invisible activity done in secret) that the Lord suddenly put a thought into her heart: *What is in your hand?*[1]

Sara relates that this was one of Glen's favorite verses, "You see God had asked the Jewish prophet Moses to lead his people, but he was too afraid to do it. Moses objected saying that the people won't trust me. They won't listen to a word I say. They're going to say, 'God appeared to him? Hardly!' So God said back, 'What is that in your hand Moses?' Moses held a shepherd's staff, so that is the simple thing God used."

She realized that what was in her hand was cardiopulmonary resuscitation (CPR) instructor's training, since she was assisting teaching CPR classes to the staff. However, retention of hospital-wide emergency preparedness skills was of great concern to her, especially since emergency medical response serviced a unique campus-based setting.

After her prayer time at lunch, Sara thought of an idea to create mock emergency scenarios and stage sudden training sessions "in the middle" of familiar scenes. *What if a heart patient collapses in the hospital cafeteria or outside? Can nurses rally strangers into action, employ bystanders, locate emergency personnel, give orders, and complete CPR? Did they know where all the phones "hung"* (landlines) *on the walls and where emergency exits were at in any location in the building?* She decided to develop mock codes to assist with the training.

Sara quickly typed up her idea; she was greeted with great excitement and acceptance from her supervisor. The nursing board was meeting that day! In fact, since this suggestion affected the entire hospital complex, she was given the 1993 Secretary's Award from the Battle Creek Veteran's Administration (VA) for nursing excellence with a hospital-wide impact. Sara marvels at how God had provided through her prayer.

She created an assessment rubric to evaluate staff preparedness, in addition to teaching correct CPR technique on Annie the CPR mannequin. Automated External Defibrillators (AEDs) were available at the VA, so AED trainers were included in the exercise.

Since Sara and I had our last chat over coffee, America was stunned by the deadliest mass shooting in our history, October 1, 2017. In minutes, a Las Vegas venue became a field of blood. I was thinking about the emergency response teams which mobilized so quickly to assist 525 plus

---

[1] Exodus 4:1–2.

injured people. Teams of professionals had seconds to think and put their training into motion. Sara likewise commented that her Bronson Hospital nursing training in the 1960s could never have imagined the daily fear that people are now facing with the recent rise in mass shooting sprees.

In Israel, a country that understands daily fear of terrorist attacks, the city hall in Tel Aviv (October 2, 2017) was lit up with the American flag and the Israeli flag, showing solidarity against the senseless terror.[2]

I had grown up hearing about *living in fear* since my grandmother and grandfather had immigrated from war-torn Feruz, Syria. My dad's Syrian father later died leaving my dad as the *head* of his family. Finding Christ as Savior as a teenager put my father on a new journey toward *shalom*. His diabetic, blind, now single, Arabic-speaking mother ran a boarding house in Detroit. My dad helped to raise his four siblings while working for Awrey Bakery. My mom's parents immigrated from the Netherlands. Not many families have a sheik, belly dancers, and klompen dancers in their lineage, yet my Christian parents established a home together in *shalom*, peace.

I asked Sara about the events in her life that led her on her journey to find *shalom*. Born and raised in a conservative Jewish family, faith was real in everyday life practices of the Goldstein family. She described how she loved the Bible stories of how God revealed Himself to His People.

She quoted Deuteronomy 6:4–9, "Hear, O Israel: The LORD our God, the LORD is one! You shall love the LORD your God with all your heart, with all your soul, and with all your strength… And these words which I command you today shall be in your heart. You shall teach them diligently to your children and shall talk of them when you sit in your house, when you walk by the way, when you lie down, and when you rise up. You shall bind them as a sign on your hand, and they shall be as frontlets between your eyes. You shall write them on the doorposts of your house and on your gates."

Sara went on to say, "My grandpa Goldstein lived with us until he died. I was five. He was a loving man who prayed and worshipped every morning with his phylacteries and prayer shawl while I quietly watched. My mother followed the kosher dietary laws, and we were very active in

---

2   Ben Ariel, "Tel Aviv city hall lit up with American Flag," (*ArutzSheva*, October 2017), http://www.israelnationalnews.com/News/News.aspx/236268

our synagogue. My four siblings and I went to Hebrew school, Sunday school, and Sabbath services. We walked to and from the synagogue on the High Holiday of Yom Kippur.

"The holidays were festive as they were always celebrating something wonderful that God had done for His People! Jewish holidays were commanded in the Bible to remember and celebrate God's faithful care. Our family was very close and drew strength from what we experienced together. I sensed God's love and presence at a very early age! Growing up, I was always troubled on Yom Kippur—the Day of Atonement—I was never assured all my sins were forgiven and my name was written in The Book of Life. The Old Testament Covenant of Moses had 613 laws to keep which was impossible. In conversations with my Christians friends, I asked them how can they be so sure you're forgiven and going to heaven? They said they believed that Jesus was not just a good man but the Son of God! It was His finished work on the cross that gave them peace and assurance.

"My hunger to know God in a very personal way kept growing stronger as I entered my teen years. I had some great friends both Jewish and Christian. I knew Jesus was a Jewish rabbi and as I begin to read the New Testament, I saw how the Old and New Testament connected to all the things my parents taught me. As I continued to seek truth, God kept showing me Jesus was more than a good man or rabbi. He was the Messiah that the Old Testament talked about.

"My favorite family holiday was Passover. Now I saw Jesus celebrating this service with His Jewish followers before His death. Instead of just reminding them to recall their exodus and deliverance from slavery.

"Likewise He also took the cup after supper, saying, 'This cup is the *new* covenant in My blood, which is shed for you'" Luke 22:20 (NKJV).

"Earlier Jesus was introduced to the Jewish people as the 'The Lamb of God who takes away the sin of the world'" (John 1:29).

"'For indeed Christ, our Passover, was sacrificed for us'" (1 Corinthians 5:7).

Decision time—December 1960

"I knew I believed facts about Jesus—but now He was calling me to trust Him as Lord and Messiah at age sixteen. So I battled with fear over what my family would say. *Would they kick me out of my home? Reject me as their daughter? Where would I go?* God pressed on my heart *You need Me more than anyone else. Trust Me with your life.* "And you will seek Me and find Me, when you search for Me with all your heart" (Jeremiah 29:13, NKJV).

"I surrendered my life to Him. When I relayed my decision with my parents, my father was very angry! He forbid me tell anyone!! I think he thought it was just a teen fad that would disappear. At least [at age sixteen] he didn't declare me dead and kick me out of the home. I was grateful! With child-like faith I asked God, *Now what do I do?*

"God gave me some wonderful Christian friends who took notes from Sunday worship services. On our bus rides to school, we started Bible memorization.

"A new verse came each week. Isaiah 26:3 NKJV was one of the first! 'You will keep him in perfect peace, whose mind is stayed on You Because he trusts in You.'

"God took good care of me! My bedroom and radio became my chapel. I would ask God questions, and he would show me answers in scripture. I didn't know how to use a concordance! I found Jesus faithful and true to His Word; my new faith was growing. I submitted to my parents' authority, and my sarcastic teenage stage was disappearing! In my first year in nursing school when no longer under my parents' authority. I said to myself, *Dear God, is now the time to make my faith public and be baptized.*"

Sara explained to me that when her parents first heard of her baptism into Christian faith, they had asked the rabbi to say the prayers for the dead. Strangely, the rabbi refused. (The rabbi gave the disclaimer that this was done in the past, but not in more modern Jewish times.) However, after her baptism, she couldn't go home for about a year and a half. That broken relationship changed when Glen wanted to meet her parents when they started dating (1964). What an answer to prayer it was to gradually see Sara's father's heart soften. He allowed her to come back home again after one and half years of being forbidden to do so. Sara said to me that she always knew that in spite of her father's religious rejection that he had always deeply loved her. Love was growing.

Sara smiled and recited, "Glen's favorite scripture was Joshua 1:7–8. Be strong and very courageous. Be careful to obey all the law my servant Moses gave you; do not turn from it to the right or to the left, that you may be successful wherever you go. Keep this Book of the Law always on your lips; meditate on it day and night, so that you may be careful to do everything written in it. Then you will be prosperous and successful."

Yes! Sara's father was instantly drawn to Glen's kind spirit, respectful manner, good listening ear and strong work ethic. She was home again for visits (1964). Since Sara had told me about her Jewish background and coming to faith, I wanted to hear about Glen's journey toward *shalom*. I did want to ask if it was connected to their choice of a name for their nonprofit ministry. Ah, for next time.

Chapter 5 Challenge: In Hebrew, God's name is *Jehovah-shalom.* According to Thomas Simcox, from Friends of Israel, God's name means "the Lord is our peace." This peace is "vertical, between God and reconciled lost humanity, and horizontal between those who have received the peace of God that surpasses human understanding."[3] What makes you feel invisible or powerless?

What can you do to prepare for eternity, which may be only a blink away?

---

[3] Simcox, 17–18.

From Accordion Music
to Maple Syrup!

Today when I came for Grogg and cookies at the cabin, I asked Sara about Glen's journey to faith. I wondered how farm life would enter the story.

Sara recalled, "Glen rededicated his life to Christ when he was a student at Michigan State. Glen's testimony also centered around the fact that he was born and raised in a Christian family. He gave his heart to Jesus when he was five. He and his mother and siblings were active at church.

"His father, Lyle Collison, had the first *self-service* Spartan store in downtown Kalamazoo, by the train station. (This was an era when gas attendants still pumped all the gas for customers!) The store was open on Sunday. Lyle didn't start attending church until after he closed his grocery business in 1974. He was a good role model for his family, moral and upright in his business practices, very kind to his customers. Many of these people did not have refrigeration, so some came to the store several times a day. He also delivered groceries to the elderly or those unable to come to Collison's Market. We did not know all these things until after his death. People shared their stories with gratitude and love." Coming from that background of compassion, Sara noted fondly, "Glen also embraced my Jewish family and loved my heritage. His steady strong faith and Bible knowledge were stabilizing factors for me. Often, he was that quiet witness through kindness and compassion."

Looking back, she can see more of God's hand of love and how he prepared Glen to work on a farm and establish a home for adults with disabilities. Glen was a member of 4-H and Future Farmers of America while attending Richland Public schools (Michigan).

This early training instilled a love for farm life and was something that Glen passed along to the Homestead residents and SHALOM network. (For example, every year they hosted cider pressing with a fall celebration.) Sara could see this love of living things on all their dates to the local county fairs (1964). Would the Creator one day use that special gift and love of living things which he gave to Glen? God was weaving a plan and putting things into Glen's hand.

In 2007, I had called Glen and asked him if he had any time to teach accordion to one of my young piano students, who also had his passion for raising goats and making cheese. Ryan Smit had come to piano lessons and expressed his desire to learn to play accordion. Well, his family was delighted to learn that they had already met Glen. Here is the story of how Glen Collison came to teach Ryan the accordion and mentor him at the Homestead, in everything from maple syrup production to farm chores, and to "oh so much more" as Ryan once put it.

My Season of Friendship with Glen Collison
by Ryan Smit

I felt like I had known Glen Collison all my life. I can remember going to the Homestead when I was little and watching him work around the farm doing various things while Mom bought eggs from his little black refrigerator on the big front porch. Mom always bought his eggs because they were not your ordinary eggs; they were farm fresh brown instead of white. At that point in time, I remember that large chain stores did not often carry brown eggs, so mom was downright thrilled to have found someone local who personally produced and sold them.

While mom was buying the eggs and talking to Glen, they would allow me to visit the various animals on the farm; mainly I loved my *friends*, the sheep. Glen saw early on that I had a keen interest in farm life and had an intense desire to learn everything that I could about it, especially through reading.

It was about eight years after we had started buying eggs from the Homestead when I found an accordion in my grandmother's attic (2005). Of course, I started playing it and began taking a few lessons from my piano teacher (Leah Wendt) who was self-taught on accordion (playing a vintage Mantovani with only 34 treble keys and 80 basses). She referred me to Glen, a talented accordion player (who was formally trained to play and who could teach Ryan how to use 41 treble keys with 120 basses!).

During these accordion lessons, Glen would ask me different questions about my interests and studies, and then he would talk to my mom.

One music lesson I remember well. We had just finished our lesson for the week and were talking about the farm while waiting for Mom to get me when Glen asked me, "What would you think about helping with chores after lessons each week?"

I remember standing there with a Cheshire grin on my face being too excited to say a word. Shortly thereafter, Mom received a nice letter from Glen asking her formal permission for me to help him on the farm with the weekly chores as part of my education. One of my fondest memories was of the first time I helped Glen in his sugar shack. The sugar shack was a building where maple sap was brought after it had been collected, and where it was also then boiled down into a final sugary product. The air was heavy with the smell of the boiling sap in the spring, intoxicating anyone who dared to enter the building. The only down side to all that heavenly smell was that the

sugar maple scent filled the air making it extremely hard to concentrate on my accordion lessons!

As maple sugaring came to an end, lambing soon commenced. This was one of Glen's favorite times out of the year. Every week there were new arrivals. It was fun watching the new lambs learn to walk while the other older lambs frisked about them. Every year it was a surprise as to how many black lambs would be born.

With the spring lambs came the unfortunate but necessary chore of docking and tagging the new arrivals. For those who are unfamiliar with sheep, tagging involves puncturing each lamb's ear in order to insert an identification tag. Docking is cutting or pinching off most of each lamb's tail thereby shortening it to a manageable and more hygienic length. While the tasks were difficult to complete, seeing the happy lambs frisking in the pasture made it well worth all the trouble.

As spring turned into summer, I struggled to keep up with Glen as we went about our farm duties. My first major accomplishment was the art of haying. Contrary to what many might think, haying is the sweatiest and hottest, dusty, painful chore ever instituted on the American farm, besides shoveling out the fuming and clucker-filled chicken coop. After one trip around the dusty and sweltering hot field, I realized that reading about farming and practicing farming involved two different things. Needless to say, that summer was the first time I ever came close to becoming as fit as I should be.

As autumn rolled around, we switched gears from haying to shearing sheep. Before this time, I had only read about shearing and also had an imaginative bias about how the sheep would behave during shearing. I am here to tell you that your view on sheep will drastically change after you are caught astride one of those two-hundred pound *haystacks on legs* while trying to bring it into the barn for shearing. And what about those movies where the sheep are being calmly sheared in the English countryside? Well, let's just say sheep have a different opinion on what their hairstyle should be and don't take it lightly when they learn that it is going to be bald! The ram was another story. No excuse was needed to butt you into next week, and the favored target made sure that you landed there on the ground.

During the afternoons in winter, we kept busy pruning apple trees in the orchard while jumping from one foot to the other to keep from feeling frozen. These excursions into the cold were somewhat warmed with the time we spent talking about the upcoming year and talking about various farming related topics. My favorite place to prune was at the Sinkovitz's orchard which Glen took care of for the owners.

That orchard had belonged to Glen's father and after this new family moved in, Glen offered his services so that the orchard would not have to be cut down or left unkempt. I loved to listen to all the stories about his childhood that he told as we stood on our ladders pruning the apple trees for the next year's crop. Over the five years that I worked for him, I learned a lot from Glen (2007-2012).

I learned farm work, baking skills, marketing tricks, accordion, and so much more. It was a privilege to work with him and become involved in SHALOM through him. Through Glen, I learned many important lessons, but none more important than that of discovering my God-given gifts and sharing them with the world around me. Thank you, Glen. From Your Friend, Ryan Smit.

After the New Year of 2012, the Smit children returned for their piano lessons on Thursday, January 5. Since the Homestead was right down the road from my piano studio, Glen graciously drove to our home that day to get Ryan to take him for his Thursday accordion lesson; his mom would pick him up from the farm after he did chores. That Thursday, Glen came and patiently waited for Ryan to pack up his accordion. He smiled at the other siblings waiting their turn for piano lessons. Musicians rehearse for performances, but the only rehearsal for the moment of death is how you have lived your whole life. Glen's family expressed it best; he kept short accounts. There were no broken relationships left behind when Glen died after an unexpected and sudden one-week illness of acute leukemia. Gratitude was also part of each day. You knew how Glen felt. The most precious things in life must be attended to on a daily basis. *Everyday matters matter every day!* As his son Michael Collison said, "On any given day, Dad was comfortable with, and to speak of, the day of his passing, claiming no regrets and no bucket list. I could always talk about death with Dad."

Glen knew that I was so happy to see Ryan playing accordion duets/gigs with him at banquets and other venues. They had played a prelude for my spring piano recital—2011.

Glen went home to be with his Lord and Savior on Saturday afternoon, January 14, 2012 at the University of Michigan Medical Center. Ryan and I had the honor of playing accordion at Glen's Funeral. What a tribute to the man who had mentored Ryan in farm life and taught him how to play. (Ryan Smit now works as a home manager, living at SHALOM Three Pines with the male residents.)

After Glen's death, Ryan gave his testimony on his baptism day at his church, saying that he finally understood the verse "Very truly I tell you, unless a kernel of wheat falls to the ground and dies, it remains only a single seed. But if it dies, it produces many seeds. Anyone who loves their life will lose it, while anyone who hates their life in this world will keep it for eternal life. Whoever serves me must follow me, and where I am, my servant also will be. My Father will honor the one who serves me" (John 12:24–26). He learned about servanthood while mentored by Glen.

After 2012, Ryan continued to work at SHALOM as a farm volunteer, using the things Glen had taught him about sheep and later working with the process of making wool dryer balls. What is a wool dryer ball? Ryan describes it well, "These fantastic little creations made of felted wool formed into a ball are designed to assist with drying clothes in the clothes dryer while reducing static electricity. The result of using this eco-friendly product is a reduction in cycle time giving you light fluffy clothes at the end of each cycle."

How do SHALOM residents make them? Again, Ryan explains the whole process so beautifully:

"The whole process of making wool dryer balls starts on the farm with the sheep and the original raw material, wool. There is a difference between using the Finland sheep and the Romney sheep. Finland sheep grow wool which is shorter in length and is quite straight, while the Romney sheep have wool which is quite a bit longer and has a tight bunch to it.

"Due to these significant wool differences, Romney sheep are better suited for the production of a wool dryer ball than the Finland sheep because its wool felts, or sticks to itself, more easily. Proper shearing also makes a large difference in the quality in the wool being used. Shearing usually takes place in early to late spring or sometimes in early autumn when it is at its prime thickness. When the shearer starts shearing, it is important that he or she keeps the blade close to the sheep being sheared and also avoids making a double cut in one area.

"Areas that are double cut consistently have hairs with shorter lengths. This is very undesirable as much of that shorter wool is then *picked out* throughout the rest of the processes.

"Much of the labor-intensive work in wool dryer ball making happens on the farm, but the time-consuming work happens at the fiber mill. Although processing wool is very time consuming, the end-product is well worth the wait. Before a fleece can be processed, it must be skirted and washed to remove all the natural oils, dirt, and other debris.

"Skirting is the process of removing the larger pieces of vegetative matter and matted wool unfit to use and must be done before the fleece can be washed. It is easily the most disliked part of wool processing. After all the wool has been cleaned, it must be run through the picker. The picker is a machine that holds the wool between two slowly turning rollers equipped with teeth while a large and quickly spinning drum covered with tines plucks out small pieces of wool.

"These pieces of wool are then hurled loosely into a large bin where they are gathered. At this point, the wool is now fit to be dyed, if a certain color is desired, or to continue through the process as naturally colored.

"The next step in the process is carding, which basically runs the wool through a series of fine combs, thereby straightening the individual hairs. The wool comes out of the carder in either of two different forms: a wide flat roll which is called a bat, or a long, loose tube called a roving. Either can be used to make the wool dryer balls, but the roving is the one most often used because it cuts down on the time needed to form each dryer ball. From start to finish, wool processing may be time-consuming but when done right, all the effort is rewarded in the end.

"The easiest part of constructing dryer balls comes when it is time to form and felt them. Dryer balls are formed by wrapping the roving into a ball, much like how one would create a ball from yarn. Once this is accomplished, these pre-dryer balls are inserted into the toe of a sock and put into a wash machine with others destined to the same fate.

"While these uncompleted dryer balls bounce around in the warm, wet interior of the wash machine, the wool bonds to itself in a process called felting. Each individual hair, in wool, is covered in tiny, microscopic scales. When these scales are warmed and rubbed together, the scales extend, and the many different hairs interlock.

"After this happens, the rinse cycle turns on, and the cooler water causes all the scales to retract, thereby locking all the hairs together permanently. The felting process complete, the dryer balls are then either left out to dry or popped into the clothes dryer for a short time. Either way, the dryer balls are then complete and ready to be put to work, rewarding those who had the patience to create them.

"SHALOM Woolery dryer balls are the result of time, effort, and high-quality wool. From the sheep to the sheared wool, to the people who process the wool and make the dryer balls, our standards show compassion and quality."

Ryan Smit offers some additional information on wool dryer balls, "Our wool dryer balls are made completely on our SHALOM farm. Our wool comes from Romney sheep raised on the farm, and their wool is processed on site also. SHALOM residents then handcraft each and every dryer ball."

After hearing about how Glen had taken up caring for sheep and teaching others, mentoring young men like Ryan, I see why Sara said Glen loved the story in Exodus 4:1–4. God performs the miracle with a simple shepherd's staff. Again, the important question here was, "What is in your hand?"

Chapter 6 Challenge: God's name is *Jehovah Raah*, The Lord is our Shepherd. This term means to "tend or to pasture."[1]

The goal of SHALOM Inc. is to enrich the lives of our residents by connecting them with the community through shepherding them in activities on our farm and empowering them to share their love of Jesus. Who have you been called to shepherd?

What is in your hand?

God can use even a simple shepherd's rod to show His authority and mighty power to deliver.

---

[1] Ibid., 18.

Another Way to Shear Sheep!

I was rather excited to find out that Glen had written a letter to the editor for Countryside Magazine. Also, I learned that he had given the magazine to Ryan Smit revealing again his efforts to mentor the young man in the art of raising sheep.

"Another way to shear sheep." Letter to the Editor by Glen Collison, 2008.[1]

Dear Countryside: Your article on shearing sheep (Jan./Feb.

 2008) was very good and correct but due to a few factors, there is another way to shear sheep. I have a small flock of nine to ten Romney ewes—the quantity is right for me, but the shearing is a problem. I wanted to keep my wool, but finding a person to shear was impossible, so I taught myself with books and videos. But my back would start scream-

---

[1] Collison, Glen. "Another way to shear sheep." *Countryside & Small Stock Journal*, May-June 2008, 50. *General OneFile.* http://0-link. galegroup.com.eaglelink.cornerstone.edu/apps/doc/A178083054/ ITOF?u=lom_cornerstc&sid=ITOF&xid=11562ed9

ing about halfway through the first or second ewe, and before we were done, we would both be on the ground.

After checking around, I found that you can shear a sheep standing on a sheep fitting stand. I had already purchased the electric clippers some years earlier, so now I bought a clutch winch fitting stand.

I get the sheep in place, then shear down the back to the belly and around the front shoulders and neck for the best wool. Then I clip all the parts I can reach, which is usually all but around the head, inside legs, some belly and some neck areas. After shearing to this point I also worm them.

Next, I back them into a heavy-duty sheep chair, which works wonderfully for getting the head, neck, inside legs, and most areas you cannot reach on the stand. It also works great for foot trimming. After all is done, I pour some delousing liquid on them.

I might add that I am sixty-six years old (2008), and do not bend like I did when I was thirty-five. Since buying the stand, we have added two goats; one is old and will not get on a milking stand but will stand on the sheep stand when it is down. I bought the goat-milking stand attachments, headpiece, and pail, and milking bench. So the stand now serves two purposes. All this holding equipment came from Sydell.

I prefer fall or late shearing as I do not have to crop the udder area in the spring. I live in southwestern Michigan where you can shear until Thanksgiving.—Glen Collison, Kalamazoo, Michigan

For a catalog of sheep and goat products and supplies, contact Sydell Inc., 46935 SD Hwy. 50, Burbank, SD 57010; 1-800-842-1369; www.sydell.com. Don't forget to mention you read about them in Countryside!

Sincerely, Glen Collison

When Ryan first told me that Glen had published an article, I was not surprised to hear that he had given the magazine to Ryan. As a senior in high school, Ryan wrote about the sheep from Glen's mentoring and doing chores at SHALOM. Ryan offers these details:

"Our sheep are an uncommon variety known as Romney. They were originally developed in Scotland and were formally recognized as a breed in the early 1800's. The Romney fleece has moderately long staple length making it excellent for many purposes. We keep two color variants, white and brown. Both are natural colors, so this allows us the ability to mix them for varying shades of white, gray, and brown.

"Residents and volunteers process all our own wool from the raw fleece. We skirt the fleece, hand-wash, pick, and card. We have machines to make rug yarn, roving, felt sheets, and batting. SHALOM Inc. also makes cat toys, roving, hot pads, and bird nesting balls. Residents are also learning to weave rugs on our looms! Our cat toys are like miniature dryer balls, and cats love them!"

After reading this, I wondered, *What does it take to run a woolery?* I learned that since the beginning (October 2012), SHALOM Woolery has had faithful volunteers. As Keith Lohman executive director outlines, "A SHALOM Woolery coach helps people successfully achieve their objectives for growth. We believe every person has value given by God that cannot be earned. We focus on the whole person, recognizing that our spiritual, emotional, physical, and relational selves all contribute to wholeness. We are learning so much from our SHALOM Woolery! We already love the sheep and wonder at their appearance after they're sheared. We have learned to *skirt* the wool, cleaning the little sticks of hay and as much dirt out of the wool as possible before its first washing. David is a constant presence at the skirting table. It is a critically important job, and nothing can happen until it's done."

SHALOM Woolery worker David says, "We have a well-lit, temperature-controlled work environment, so even though skirting is demanding, the surroundings are great. We take time almost every day for a short nature walk too. Oh my goodness, it will be fantastic when we have our new SHALOM Woolery building built. Skirting is the most 'fun' job. Each fleece is unique in the color of the wool and the way it feels."

There are many rinses after washing to get all the soap out. It takes one or two people to haul out the dirty water and add in the fresh water until the wool is as clean as possible. Lou, Gretchen, and Cindy, three of our great volunteers, help ensure that the wool is thoroughly rinsed. Calvin and Gideon haul water out many times for every batch of wool.

Pastor Lohman wrote, "Gideon comes from the community and is a cheerful hard worker."

Gideon tells us, "I think the SHALOM Woolery is awesome! It's good, hard work and a lot of fun. I like the washing machine work best of all so far."

Calvin added, "I've done all the SHALOM Woolery jobs to get the wool all ready to use. I like the washing and rinsing and hauling out the used water as I'm a strong man. I can take the water out and dump it easily. Every month I make dryer balls and cat toys too!"

Once the wool is spun in the old washing machine, Jim and anyone available separates the wool loosely and lays it out to dry overnight. Hearing more of their wool production story, I was soon to learn that this dream of making wool balls and wool products for residents to sell did not materialize fully until after Glen's passing (January 14, 2012). Glen was first to develop the dryer ball product. He learned how to run the wool machines, which also included the picker, carder, yarn maker, and felting machine. He processed wool to make the dryer balls and wool products but also did the weaving and spinning with wool. SHALOM Inc. purchased the Homestead sheep flock in 2012 and then leased Homestead Farm and Wool Processing Equipment. Glen's son Michael would later note, "I can think of no better metaphor of my dad's life at this time than his weavings. He wove a deliberate life that was colorful, unconventional, and spirited."

The SHALOM Woolery was established October 2012. Also in 2012, our training began in Apple Creek, Ohio, at the Morning Star Fiber Mill for wool processing.[2] In the fall of 2011, Sara and Glen had gone there for wool production training and attended a conference on processing wool fiber as a sustainable business. Thus, Glen's early efforts had been the forerunner to bring the Woolery to SHALOM. Sara firmly believes God had been weaving His Master Design all along. Sara notes that Glen's death was a sudden crisis which turned the tide for the farm's direction. His son Michael Collison confirms, "Two days beyond the burial and funeral celebration of life, I finally ventured out to the small barns and buildings. I am not a big animal lover, yet I did appreciate his passion for them. My dad's sheep stared at me, and my eyes swelled with tears. *Sheep without their shepherd.*"

Had Glen been given a different diagnosis, perhaps a long or lingering illness, Sara said she *knew* Glen would have sold the whole farm and the sheep, thinking he would not want to leave her behind with so much responsibility. SHALOM Woolery was the seed of life that grew out of death. Again, the Bible verse Ryan loved returned in full force: "Very truly I tell you, unless a kernel of wheat falls to the ground and

---

2 Andrea Zippay, "Morning Star Fiber Mill turns wool, alpaca fleeces into profitable wares," 2008, Farm and Dairy, https://www.farmanddairy.com/news/morning-star-fiber-mill-turns-wool-alpaca-fleeces-into-profitable-wares/9504.htm

dies, it remains only a single seed. But if it dies, it produces many seeds."[3] Five years later, 2017, you can see the fruit grow. Pastor Keith Lohman writes:

From the beginning, the "product" of the SHALOM Woolery has been increasing wholeness for individuals who live with significant challenges and brokenness in their lives. We confess we are all broken people, finding our wholeness in Jesus Christ. Work is a gift of God (Genesis 2:15) meant to be life giving, stimulating and fulfilling.

The work, however, is to be the context, not the end goal, of life blessed by God, the abundant life of *shalom* (peace).

At the SHALOM Woolery, production is measured differently than the world's measure and has more to do with the work of God in us than production measured by our world.

Work is to be an expression of what God is perfecting in us, bringing Him the profits through glory, honor, and growth as disciples of Jesus. The SHALOM Woolery is all about people of different abilities working together in community, learning new skills, thriving in an encouraging atmosphere, growing mentally, relationally, emotionally, and spiritually, while receiving wholeness from beyond ourselves.

"Baa Baa black sheep, have you any wool?" Well, exactly how much wool is "three bags full?" Since opening in October 2012, The SHALOM Woolery has learned that it takes a *lot* of wool to keep that busy! So how many sheep does it take to supply the SHALOM Woolery for one year? The current (2017) answer is 100 sheep.

About ten percent of our wool comes from SHALOM sheep, and the rest is donated or purchased locally. If you know someone with sheep, ask what they do with all their wool. SHALOM can put it to good use.

---

[3] John 12:24–26.

What do we make with all that wool more than three bags full? Variety! We make rugs, hats, dryer balls, cat toys, nesting balls, hot pads, art work, bookmarks, yarn, rug yarn, and felt sheets.

Our products sell locally in Kalamazoo, Michigan, at the SHALOM Thrift Store (6276 Riverview Drive), and at Wings Stadium Event Center, Sawall Health Foods, Natural Health Center, Wild Birds Unlimited, People's Co-op, and Zeilinger Wool Company (Frankenmuth) Green Scene of Marshall, Michigan, and the Farmer's Markets in Kalamazoo and Portage, Michigan.

We have twenty-nine participants who worked 260 days in April 2017!

We also had nine community volunteers and four staff who worked the SHALOM Woolery at various times during the week, spring 2017.

Wool dryer balls are our best seller and take the most wool. They weigh one point eight ounces each. In 2016, we produced 2,211 which took 249 pounds of washed wool. Before it was skirted and washed, that would have been approximately 500 pounds of sheared wool on our skirting tables! This does not account for nearly 200 pounds of fleece used for the variety of other projects. Sometimes we even have black wool, but that is rare. Maybe that's why the Baa Baa Black Sheep was happy to have three bags full.[4] You can support SHALOM by your presence!

Your church, group, or family can adopt a SHALOM home!

---

[4] "Baa Baa Black Sheep," *Sheep 101. info*, accessed November 9, 2017, http://www.sheep101.info/black.html

We are looking for additional support for each of our homes as a form of outreach and service in partnership with our home care providers. Think about it! Adopting a home could mean planning an occasional activity night for residents or attending an event together. It could mean making donations of needed personal items, throwing a party or picnic, or offering recreation, such as a game night. There might be projects around the house that need attention. Care providers need a break and can always use some time away—a free afternoon or evening for a date or shopping would be so beneficial! This would be such fun and guaranteed to be a growing experience and blessing for all. We can connect you and help get started! We are always looking for more faithful community volunteers to help us achieve our goals! Please come and visit Monday–Thursday, 10 a.m.–2 p.m. any time! Closed for holidays and snow days!

SHALOM Worship welcomes you! At Worship, you can meet many residents and care providers, board members, and friends of SHALOM. Plus we believe you will be deeply blessed and encouraged in your walk with the Lord.

SHALOM does not make any grandiose claims about our worship experience. But we do have something unique and very special. If you are looking for real life, for acceptance, for a welcoming and comforting place, please come! You don't need to dress up too much. We worship in the long red Shepherd's Barn! And it's Saturday night. Relax.

This worship is for everyone, for people challenged with disabilities, for their families, and for those who just need a deeper wholeness.

We meet the first Saturday of each month, 6:30 p.m. at the Shepherd's Barn, 6276 N. Riverview Dr., 1 1/2 miles north of "G" Ave. Come, experience SHALOM!

Chapter 7 Challenge: Jesus's name is The Good Shepherd (John 10): "I am the good shepherd. The good shepherd lays down his life for the sheep. The hired hand is not the shepherd and does not own the sheep. So when he sees the wolf coming, he abandons the sheep and runs away."

Who have you been called to shepherd? Do you follow Jesus's example?

CHAPTER 8

If Only These *Walls* Could Talk!

This week, Ryan Smit's siblings came to piano lessons and gave me a book: *If Only the Walls Could Talk*. The Collisons' Homestead is mentioned in this history book highlighting the architectural heritage of Cooper, Michigan:

The Homestead house (purchased by Sara and Glen Collison in 1987) at 6191 North Riverview Drive was built by Patrick Bunbury. Mr. Bunbury purchased forty acres in 1834, and soon after, eighty acres. Because of his ability and hard work, he cleared one of the largest farms in Cooper Township and was a most successful farmer. Patrick Bunbury served the Cooper community as township assessor, school inspector, and as a justice of the peace. Mr. Bunbury was also very devoted to his church.[1]

To put this extraordinary feat into a broader historical context, Michigan would not become a state until January 26, 1837 when the

---

[1] Ward Christlieb, *If Only the Walls Could Talk: The Architectural Heritage of Cooper, Michigan,* (Allegan Forest, MI: The Priscilla Press, 2000), 63.

local paper called for a "jollification" to celebrate the long-awaited push for statehood![2] Since the book's account also mentioned local public library records, I went internet surfing and found out that Mr. Bunbury mortgaged the farm to loan money to help his church build a new church building. Unfortunately, the loan was never repaid.[3]

However, I still found the account very moving since this industrious farmer had set the sill (foundation) for future generations. If the Homestead walls on Riverview Drive *could talk*, they might tell a story about Patrick Bunbury, a faith-filled farmer whose investment established a church which eventually founded Borgess Hospital in Kalamazoo, Michigan.

I was reminded of a Bible verse when I heard about Patrick Bunbury's generous gifts, his industrious farm work, and his good deeds which eventually culminated in building a hospital: "God is not unjust, he will not forget your work and the love you have shown him as you have helped his people and continue to help him."[4]

In the summer of 1987, Glen and Sara took on the heavy labor and spent six months refurbishing this 1834 Michigan Farmhouse in Cooper Township. Their family and *an army of volunteers* made up the work crews! Dr. Dee Crittenden echoes, "No growth can ever be accomplished without the army of volunteers who make the impossible dream a reality over and over again."[5]

After the dedication on October 12, 1987 by Pastor Roy Ackermann, the newly dedicated "Homestead" on 6191 North Riverview Drive received its first two residents, Hope and Karen. I learned from reading Glen and Sara's memory album entry on October 12, 1987 that Hope had raised goats too!

Speaking of her new family at the Homestead, Karen wrote, "Thank you, Glen and Sara for letting me live in your home. You let me stand on my own two feet." I do remember seeing Karen's photo on a commemorative wheaties box displayed at our local Parchment, Michigan Hardings Market: 1998 Michigan Outstanding Special Olympian!

---

2   *Kalamazoo Gazette*, February 11, 1837.
3   Fred Peppel, "St. Augustine's: In spite of Everything," Kalamazoo Public Library, http://www.kpl.gov/local-history/religion/st-augustines.aspx
4   Hebrews 6:10, NKJV.
5   Dr. Dee Crittenden, "A Celebration of Service in God's Love, 20th Anniversary," 2007, SHALOM, Inc. Kalamazoo, MI.

The Original 1987 Homestead on Riverview Drive grew from one to two homes with the addition of Homestead South in 1988. This was run by the Collisons' daughter, Julie as part of her EFE (Education for Employment) Program while she was still a Parchment High School Senior (and she graduated with honors). God miraculously provided this home with the encouragement of Igo and Elizabeth Augustins. At age eighteen, Julie felt the call of God on her life to become a caregiver and to manage her own home. She became the "sister" to six ladies at Homestead South. Julie's Grandmother Goldstein was moving to Minneapolis and had provided the majority of furnishings for Julie's AFC home.

Julie was absent briefly while Barry and Michelle Broadhurst and family served there. With a sudden severe retinal tear in Glen's eye in 2003, Julie (Kortz) Stevens and sons Calvin, Noah, and Brendan moved back into the Homestead to help Glen and Sara to care for eleven residents. (Julie and Doc Stevens live with the residents at the Original Homestead, 2018.)

In 2003, Tom and Audrey Youngblood and their three children came to help and later bought the Homestead South in 2005 which continues to 2018. Fred and Cheryl Heckman also provided respite care for the Homesteads and eventually opened *Cornerstone* in 1993, which closed in 2013, three years after Fred's death.

By 1990, the Homestead grew to include another home, Homestead North (which would later become SHALOM Three Pines). Now with three Homestead homes serving adult residents with developmental disabilities, Glen and Sara realized that an organization was needed in order to secure this ministry's future service to our most vulnerable population. They were blessed to meet people like Edna and Harry Meier whose family member Bob would live at SHALOM. People recall that Edna was "filled with joy, had a wonderful smile, and had strong faith in the Lord."[6] Both Edna and Harry were passionately involved in working to reform laws pertaining to special needs children. They supported Glen and Sara, embracing the vision for the future.

On June 13, 1990, S.H.A.L.O.M. Inc was established as a 501(c)(3) nonprofit organization. Self Help Alternative Living Opportunities of Michigan is a most creative acronym. How did the Collisons find this title for their life's work?

---

[6] Edna Meier, http://obits.mlive.com/obituaries/kalamazoo/obituary.aspx?pid=168811383.

Well, let's ask some other questions first. What if the Collisons had spotlighted their own name by calling it "The Collison Homestead"? What if they had given their own name to the nonprofit organization they founded COLLISONS Inc.? They did not because another purpose was guiding them.

Glen and Sara were just like the famous Christian businessman Henry Parsons Crowell, who picked a name for his business to highlight the providence of God. Like the Collisons, Crowell was a man "hungry for the Word of God."[7] Crowell viewed his whole business project as a response to obeying the Word and an answer to a specific prayer.

Like the Collisons, Henry Parsons Crowell bought a property in poor shape but gave the whole risky endeavor to the Lord. Crowell's keen marketing skills turned America's perception of oats from horse food to a nutritious option, branding it as *America's Breakfast Cereal.* Many people have heard of Quaker Oats, but few know the name of its godly founder, Henry Parsons Crowell. Henry had prayed and made a promise to God to keep his name out of the title if God would be pleased to bless his floundering Quaker oat mill. He soon became a very wealthy man, but kept his prayer promise and gave God the glory by keeping his name out of the title. Henry Parsons Crowell (Quaker Oats founder) Grant Money still funds International Missions Projects, so his legacy for the gospel continues to this day.[8]

From a condemned property to a thriving ministry, God also blessed Glen and Sara. They initiated this model for home care to better assist adults with disabilities to find new abilities in a home context with Christian families. They gave their dream to the Lord in answer to their prayer for wisdom. They purposefully chose SHALOM Inc.'s name after a season of prayer. Sara tells the story:

"God surely gave us our name. I was praying while driving to work on the day before we were to meet with my mother's attorney to file our incorporation papers. I wanted a biblical name that incorporated my Jewish heritage, had meaning, but would be understood by most people. God spoke into my heart: *Shalom!* I loved the sound of it.

"My normal routine was to read a brief passage from scripture in the morning before I got out of my car at work. I had been reading in the book of Hebrews, so I started to read again where I had read last. The

---

7   Henry Parsons Crowell, "Quaker Oats," Giants for God, accessed October 31, 2017, http://www.giantsforgod.com/henry-parsons-crowell-quaker-oats/

8   See the following website, http://crowelltrust.org/about-us/

verse was Hebrews 13:20 'Now may the God of peace—there was that name again—*shalom, peace!*' Not only was the name confirmed, but the promised blessings in verses twenty and twenty-one were so powerful. This expressed our mission and our purpose in one word—*shalom.* Now I was really excited and couldn't wait to get home to Glen and tell him!

"Upon arrival at home, I quickly blurted out, 'I think God gave us our nonprofit organization's name today—*Shalom!*'

"Glen got a big grin on his face and said, 'There is a letter that came today. Look on the desk. Read it.'

"The letter began, 'Shalom! You don't know me, but...' (It was a letter from the Goodwill supervisor for one of our first residents. She was thanking us for the wonderful care we had given to her client!)

"Now this was the third time I had heard *Shalom* in the same day. First, God spoke in my heart; then second, He spoke through His living word, and third, through the words of a stranger!

"As a follow-up, we wanted to meet this supervisor, so we invited her to dinner a few weeks later. We asked her if she was Jewish, thinking maybe that was why she used the *shalom* greeting.

"She said *no,* and that she wasn't really sure why she had used the word in the letter. As we talked, we learned that she was from the Kalamazoo community and lived on North Rose Street.

"Excited, I said 'My grandparents Jacob and Rachel Goldstein lived on North Rose Street, years ago. He was a shoe cobbler.'

"By now her eyes were getting very large as she responded amazed, 'My apartment is behind your grandparents' house. I live in the old shoe shop.'"

Shalom can be translated from Hebrew to mean "The place where God's will is being done!" Hebrews 13: 20 & 21 clearly defines it.

Now may the God of peace (*shalom*) who brought up our Lord Jesus from the dead, that great Shepherd of the sheep, through the blood of the everlasting covenant, make you complete in every good work to do His will, working in you what is well pleasing in His sight, through Jesus Christ, to whom be glory forever and ever. Amen.

In Glen's own words, "God gave us purpose—God's peace was to be shared with adults with disabilities and their families so that wholeness was their reality."

As I drove up to the farm for our coffee chat today, a forecast of possible snow overshadowed our late fall morning writing session at the cabin.

I knew Sara's cabin fireplace would make it cozy, and the Highlander Grogg would be brewing. I was looking forward to hearing more about her Goldstein side of the family who had once lived on the Homestead property. What a unique connection to the same land.

I had also read in Sara's prayer journal notes that as a child, she had gone down the steps in a stroller but stopped miraculously in front of the glass plate entrance to an apartment building—what amazing providence!

In the summer of 1946, at age two, little Sara was being taken for a walk on a cool windy day with her older siblings, Ray and Marilyn. (The Goldstein children: Rosalind, 1938; Raymond, 1941; Marilyn, 1942; Sara [Collison], 1944; and Adina, 1955.) As they were walking past a local construction site, a gust of wind suddenly swirled around them and caused one of the kerosene smudge pots to flare up. Suddenly, a spark landed on her lightweight cotton pants, and she was on fire! (These heavy round kerosene pots were filled with kerosene and had a wick surrounded by a safety cage. They were mostly used for construction sites or railroad crossings.)

Sara says thankfully, "Our neighbor Pat saw me and rushed to pat out the flames with her own bare hands. I was later aware of the fact that my little wool coat had rescued my life. The flames were retarded by the natural fibers of the wool. My mid body section and neck were safely protected by my wool coat, but I was left with third degree burns on my right leg and left hand."

How ingenius of the Lord to design sheep wool to be weather-resistant and fire retardant. The *Handbook of Fire Resistant Textiles* affirms, "Wool is naturally flame retardant. It does not ignite easily, burns with a self-extinguishing flame, and forms a soft dissipating ash residue whereas synthetic fibers form a hard, molten bead residue with melt-drip behavior. Wool is preferred since it presents fewer hazards for industrial and military uses in furnishings and apparel."[9]

What a miracle indeed! Our Creator God had preserved Sara, his little lamb, using the wool. In later school years, she would be teased

---

[9] J. M. Cardamone, "Flame Resistant Wool and Wool Blends," Woodhead Publishing Series in Textiles, 2013, https://www.sciencedirect.com/science/article/pii/B9780857091239500092

about her *scar leg*. Was this the start of God's healing in her life to later give her such great compassion for those who were suffering? Would her love for the miracle of wool one day grow too? Yes!

As I sat at her table today, Sara showed me the handwoven mats made by Glen and the residents. Wool art pieces are displayed everywhere.

She taught me that "Wool is very forgiving. The fibers felt together for greater strength. This quality aids their individual weaknesses. You see we share greater strength in community while we are weaker alone. You can shape and reshape wool as it felts together and becomes more beautiful. Fiber crafts from wool make a perfect match for our adult residents."

I had to agree as I looked at the wool crafts everywhere. Well, little Sara, rescued by the wool, still had a long recovery in 1946, being hospitalized for surgery and infection after this burn accident.

Her parents were fearful for her life and surrendered her back to God. She would later recover and also survive rheumatic fever at age six, but only after missing a year of school. Her mom tutored her while family and friends visited, making the long trip to the Ann Arbor Hospital. I can surely see how these early events in her life created a deep bond of love with her parents.

Later in 1963, when Sara's Jewish father was greatly upset by her decision to be baptized and publicly follow Christ, Sara recalls that, "My mom would not interfere because I was given back to God when I was burned at age two. She had dedicated me to God seventeen years earlier!"

Sara beamed, "You see, Leah, not a single experience is wasted in God's kingdom. Can you look at your life to see the stepping stones getting connected? I just had a wonderful time studying the book of Esther with our Bible study class on Wednesday night [Haven Church, Kalamazoo, Michigan]. Mordecai, the cousin of Queen Esther respectfully sat at the gate in a leadership role. He was not just listening for gossip. He was on duty, doing God's bidding. The first murder plot Mordecai overheard and stopped was against King Xerxes. Mordecai was never publicly honored for that. Next, Haman the Prime Minister of Persia plotted to kill all the Jews, but God intervened with a most unique plot twist. One night, King Xerxes could not sleep. He ordered the book of the chronicles, a record of his reign, to be read to him. Suddenly, he discovered that Mordecai had not been honored for exposing Bigthana and Teresh, two of his officers who guarded the doorway, who had conspired to assassinate him. The credit for the good deed was greatly delayed. There was no parade for daily obedience, but God had already arranged the timing for the reward, and also for the rescue of all the Jewish people. God took Haman, the very person who plotted to kill the Jews and made him honor Mordecai the Jew, in a public parade!

In Esther chapter 6, we read more of the story with the ironic twist: Haman had thought to himself, *Who is there that the king would rather honor than me?* So, he decided that for the man the king delights to honor, they should bring a royal robe that the king has worn and a horse the king has ridden, one with a royal crest placed on its head. Then the robe and horse should be entrusted to one of the king's most noble princes. Let them robe the man the king delights to honor and lead him on the horse through the city streets, proclaiming before him that this is what is done for the man the king delights to honor!

The King commanded Haman to go at once and get the robe and the horse and do just as he had suggested for Mordecai the Jew, who sat at the gate! God had planned a public parade for the private obedience of Mordecai. (*If walls could talk, they would have shouted his name like a victory chant! Mordecai, Mordecai, Mordecai!*)

The rather harsh circumstances were more like a series of quiet daily steps down this path of favor to great blessings. Sara suggested firmly, "If we do not obey, God will put us on a shelf and find another to fulfill his plan. Either way, his plan step by step unfolds, like it did for Esther. Glen and I realized that we just had to obey God."

Sara went on to tell me that this was one of her favorite holidays as a child, the Jewish Feast of Purim in the month of March. At the synagogue, the Rabbi would take out the Megillah (book of Esther) scroll from its container to read it. When the name of wicked Haman was read, everyone boos, stomps, and wildly shakes noisemakers (graggers) to blot out the sound of his name!

She offered me a special cookie which she had made just for last night's Bible study on Queen Esther: Hamantaschens. The Hebrew word means "Haman's hat." The circle of sugared dough is folded into

SARA L. COLLISON AND LEAH M. WENDT

a triangle and filled with a wonderful date filling. She also made some cherry ones to go with our morning coffee.

While we were meeting, Sara was bustling about brewing large pots of coffee for the morning volunteer workers at SHALOM.

She did not need to, but she apologized for *interrupting* our discussion with trips back and forth to her kitchen counter, prepping a large amount of coffee. I thought of a favorite quote from C.S. Lewis, "The great thing, if one can, is to stop regarding all the unpleasant things as interruptions of one's *own*, or *real* life. The truth is, of course, that what one calls the interruptions are precisely one's real life—the life God is sending one day by day; what one calls one's *real life* is a phantom of one's own imagination."[10]

Life at SHALOM seems to require this oxymoron of *structured flexibility* to accept interruptions as part of a daily rhythm. Caregivers are on call and intercede or intervene with ease for this community of adults. For the residents, the end outcome is stronger with a family than without. This is what Glen knew.

Well, the volunteers this morning had been working on the foundation for a new pavilion and digging holes to set posts, but water had filled in their work and sides were collapsing in little mud slides. This is physically grueling work, but they stood up to the challenge!

Sara showed me a text message with an update, "Consumer's delivered ready mix. Inspector could not *see* our work under water. So pumping water out to *prove* our work. Three to four people digging today after pumping water out. Some raise, some brace, align, then plumb, a methodical work team… just refreshing to get something into the air away from the mud."

As I sat there eating little Haman's hats, I could see how the beautiful buildings for SHALOM represented so many volunteers with this same team spirit. Sara explained how building something new for God is still very much like it was in Esther's ancient biblical time: we face hardships, discouragements, opposition, uphill battles, and physical struggles. She remembers a time when they applied for a grant but as a new fledgling nonprofit organization, they were turned down and told they had to *prove their work* first. They persevered.

---

[10] *The Quotable Lewis.* (Wheaton, IL: Tyndale House Publishers, 1989), 335.

86

Where did the Collisons glean this strength that they share with those volunteers who have worked so hard for thirty years to build up this ministry? Their source of hope is the Word of God. Sara mentioned how Glen loved listening to J. Vernon McGee speak on Queen Esther. He had even bought the set of his commentaries. The workers, supporters, and volunteers have been obedient, like Queen Esther, for "for such a time as this." I could see those *simple daily steps of obedience* in proving and building up a ministry.

Just read the list: "Ongoing SHALOM network Community Life" 2017.

1. SHALOM Woolery: Open Monday to Thursday, 10 a.m. to 2 p.m.
2. Farm Team Gardening, animal care and projects Monday–Thursday from 10 a.m. to 2 p.m.
3. Connection Depot Thrift Store, open every Friday and Saturday, 9 to 3 p.m.
4. SHALOM worship. First Saturday of each month, 6:30 p.m.
5. Network Meal: 6:00 p.m. second Tuesday of each month.
6. Care Provider Gathering, monthly.
7. Movie/Activity Night, Last Monday, monthly, 6:15 p.m.

8. Board Meeting, monthly
9. AKTION club (Kiwanis) 5:00 p.m. third Tuesday, monthly.
10. Holiday Picnics and gatherings.
11. Community Trip/Camping: September. Tri-Camp Labor Day.
12. New Year's Party (December 31)
13. Spring Gardening (May to September)
14. Maple Syrup Production from our trees, in Sugar Shack, March.
15. Grape Harvest and Jelly, September.
16. Apple picking and cider press—October
17. Community/ Farm Open House (June, October)
18. Friday Night Out (eat out and go to the YMCA)
19. First Youth FARM Camp offered to the Community (2017)

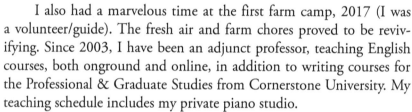

I also had a marvelous time at the first farm camp, 2017 (I was a volunteer/guide). The fresh air and farm chores proved to be revivifying. Since 2003, I have been an adjunct professor, teaching English courses, both onground and online, in addition to writing courses for the Professional & Graduate Studies from Cornerstone University. My teaching schedule includes my private piano studio.

I greatly benefited from that beautiful week of sunshine, time *off the grid*, a few hours away from computer screens to collect chicken eggs, harvest vegetables, and learn Bible stories, work in a garden, pet alpacas or walk goats, and enjoy a hayride with our granddaughter. We shared walks and talks while feeding farm animals and making wool crafts, joyfully intereacting with adult residents with developmental disabilities who live on the farm. I went back to teaching renewed and refreshed! Looking back, I can see how quickly SHALOM grew. Here is the director's 2010 Praise Report:

1. New Shepherd's Barn Activity Center (May). 2. Monthly Shalom Network Meals at the Barn 3. Opened Connection Depot Thrift Store (July) 4. Built Barn Porch roof on east parking side

The 2011 Highlights include a new SHALOM Network Movie night, 1. Growing Grace Home purchased (May) 2. Connection Link Camp, First annual at Warner Camp (June) 3. Charter Kalamazoo Aktion Club (July) 4. SHALOM Three Pines Home Garage built & Front Porch on Shepherd's Barn.

Sara echoed joyfully, "My father would be so honored to see all that has been accomplished on his land for this work. You see, my father had bought the original property [190 acres] back in 1934 as he was in real estate."

At this point, I was curious to ask if she was born on this land and did she or any of her relatives live here. How did the land transfer from your father or the other investors to you and Glen? I realized I had just bombarded her with a myriad of questions. Wouldn't Patrick Bunbury love to hear all about this too!

Sara pointed out, "You know our Heavenly father was really watching over us when we were living on the *back side of the wilderness* during our years at the Ottawa County Farm. Before we could come to the Homestead in 1987, God had to first teach us some lessons. We did not know that The Homestead was waiting for us. However, God knew. We were just like the three million Jews which God fully planned on preserving by uncovering Haman's plot. It is rather astounding how God used just *one* obedient man and *one* obedient woman!"

Chapter 8 Challenge: God cares for the weakest of the weak because he is the strongest of the strong. God's name in Hebrew is *El Elyon*: This name refers to the Most High God, affirming "the Lord as the strongest strong one; the highest high one; the most powerful, powerful one. In Hebrew, repeating the same word (*El, El*) indicates the superlative, the best, the highest i.e., Song of Songs (Solomon). Do you feel sometimes that you are just *talking to the walls* or that no one is listening or that no one sees your steps of obedience? Seek *El Elyon*.[11] Brother Lawrence (1614 to 1691) instructs us, "You need not cry very loud; he is nearer to us than we are aware of." [12]

---

[11] Simcox, 17–18.

[12] Brother Lawrence, "Prayer Resources," Prayer Coach, May 18, 2011, sponsored by Josiah's Covenant, all rights reserved, https://prayer-coach.com/prayer-resources/

CHAPTER 9

Transitions Are Messy!

During the busy week after Thanksgiving, Sara and I did not meet. She and I were both "transitioning" to holiday mode, packing away one season and getting out the boxes for the next one. We spoke briefly over the phone since we were both exhausted. I missed our Thursday appointment due to a cold and an extra-long work list for the holiday. Sara was ready to pack up the Grogg and deliver it to my door to cheer me up!

She observed comfortingly, "Leah, I have come to learn that life is unpredictable. Transitions are messy. You just have to roll up your sleeves and commit to the present task even when facing an unknown future. You have to move in the Spirit and just be still and listen. In the morning, I wake up and ask God what he wants me to do this day: Lord, give me the schedule, the order, the wisdom. For instance, when I told you our wedding story, I prayed about how to share that story completely, just as it happened. Why? God had designed Glen for his purposes, and now I could covet another person's life or be bitter toward God about taking Glen, just like anyone else could become bitter about losing their sons or husbands to war. Here is the question: Do we really trust God with our whole life?"

I was beginning to see what she meant. Glen's father had been a World War II prisoner of war for one year, captured in Germany when Glen was two years old (1943). God had intervened already by establishing a plan created just for Glen. His dad lived. (Sara mentioned again that this made Glen very patriotic too.) Their son Michael elaborates, "Who, but God, could have imagined shaping the lives of a young nurse and a grocer with a green thumb to create a life-giving Christian community that cares holistically for the developmentally disabled. The narrative of SHALOM is entwined with the stories of *personal* spiritual journey that challenge and inspire our own faith."

When Sara had mentioned on the phone that she would be setting up her Christmas Village, I had no idea that her display takes her weeks to set up because it has hundreds of pieces and multiple tiers placed around three different venues in the room! The village symbolically mirrors each phase of their life together on the farm. Sara and Glen had started this village when they lived at the Ottawa County Farm (1978–1987 Michigan) when their little kids made hand-painted pieces and fired them in a kiln.

Their elegant collection even has a candle-making section and a maple sugar shack. I just love the idea of a mini Christmas tree farm in a Christmas village, but I later learned that Glen's dad actually raised Christmas trees, thousands of them!

She also told me how Glen enjoyed setting up all the tables and the various platform levels. The display wraps around the living room and into the "Glory Room." The last year that Glen set it up in December 2011, they joked about leaving it up until Valentine's Day and letting it get dusty. (Glen passed away in January 14, 2012, so Sara left it up far longer than Easter. That was a hard year of shock, grief, and transitions in a new stage of life.)

Sara relayed again, "You see, Leah, we are so fearful in transitions. We run from hard things. So many people say they believe, but they must transition forward from mere belief to *trust*. The children of Israel were content to stay in bondage in Egypt, but God had to take them into the wilderness and teach them to trust Him! Are we really willing to do that, trust God with our whole life, no matter what happens?"

I could really see that the holidays bring up these hard questions of change and loss. Just looking at the faces missing from around a family table, people long for a celebration with all the loved ones reunited together again.

Sara told me, "This Christmas village has pieces mirroring the different stages of our life together and reminds me of the millennial kingdom, where the Messiah will rule and reign. We will worship, live, play, and work happily, eternally together, all united, sharing in perfect *shalom!*"

I look forward to seeing this family heirloom village, drinking Highlander Grogg, and praying together. I may even do some extra studying on the topic of the millennium so I can connect to the significance and understand more of what she means by the biblical millennium of global peace. Until then, I too am trying not to get rundown in the added excitement and rush to host a family reunion in honor of our son's upcoming doctoral graduation.

I was out shopping at our local Harding's Village Market when I met a resident from SHALOM. His smile broke through my busy mode with a peaceful transition. Jerry, my bagger, carefully handed me my carton of eggs very politely, "You will need to hold these eggs. They are delicate things."

As we chatted about eggs, I told him about our granddaughter who wants to raise chickens, but we cannot do that. Jerry just kindly suggested that I should bring her down to SHALOM and told me when, where, and how I could find SHALOM and buy nice, fresh brown eggs for her and see farm animals too.

Instantly, I could see exactly what Sara and Glen were accomplishing. They had learned to intercede on behalf of this underserved population and had taught them how to turn obstacles into simple stepping stones. Jerry's response illustrated the teachings from his SHALOM home.

Pastor Keith Lohman, the executive director of SHALOM Inc. since 2007 explains, "Glen helped people become more self-sufficient and more confident in their abilities. Glen always focused on what people could do rather than what they could not do."

Later in the week, I was out in our community and was greeted by Matthew, another SHALOM friend, who recognized me from playing the piano at Haven Church (Kalamazoo, Michigan).

He asked me, "So what did you do this weekend, Leah?"

I mentioned that I had worked outside in our garden and did some fall yardwork. He went on to inquire, "Well, are you good at it? Do you like doing it? Maybe you should do it some more next weekend, and that is how you will get very good at it."

Not surprisingly, I could see again the training by repetition and love pouring through those words: *Focus on what you can do, not on what you cannot do.* At church on Sunday, I was greeted by another SHALOM resident, Tracey. She gave me a joyful hug as she recognized me from helping at SHALOM Farm Camp, 2017. She laughed when I later told her that we had just gotten a new dryer, and I almost forgot to get the wool dryer balls out of the old one before the Geek Squad came and hauled it away. She told me she had been busy weaving mats and assured me that I could probably get plenty of new dryer balls. How did they gain this joy in work?

Judy Vlietstra, a SHALOM volunteer and wife of Phil, explains this transition quite nicely, "For some of the residents, living at SHALOM is the first time they have been around other people that are a lot like themselves. The faith these residents have is astounding. Glen and Sara Collison have made it their life's mission to teach them about the Bible with every task, be it setting the table or cleaning a chicken coop. They have obeyed the commandment from Deuteronomy 6:9, 'And these words which I command you today shall be in your heart. You shall teach them diligently to your children and shall talk of them when you sit in your house, when you walk by the way, when you lie down, and when you rise up.' They have taught them to their residents, their own children, and now their children's children as well."

Marcy, a SHALOM Woolery Coach (2017) similarly notes, "I see lonely people not lonely anymore, fellowshipping while hand cleaning the wool, high-fiving each other when reaching a work goal. I hear phone orders for dryer balls, the farm team sharing prayer requests, residents learning memory verses, and I watch rugs taking shape while others learn to weave on looms. Come and see how good God is! In a sentence, it is all about growing toward wholeness and discipleship through the love of Jesus."

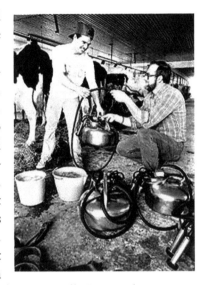

However, this transition for residents to have happier, more productive, fulfilled lives does not happen overnight. As for Sara and Glen, they too had to transition their skills set "to learn to deal with special needs people of all ages, handle emergencies, work with state agencies, give solid input, grow food and preserve it well, listen to residents, care for residents and family members" as their friend Dr. Dee Crittenden further explains about their ministry. Apparently, the transition process from their former position was what Sara calls "Messy but we can see God's justice right in the pain. God has to bring us to himself first and get our attention. He knows the obstacles in our relationships. For us, he used Ottawa Community Haven—the poor farm."

In 1978, Glen was hired as full-time farm assistant at the Community Haven while Sara through a temp service worked every other weekend as relief nursing administrator for sixty adults with disabilities. The Collisons' children were welcomed to join their parents at work. Glen and Sara began living at the Ottawa Community Haven Farm (now the Eastmanville Farm Park on the Grand River in Polkton Township, Michigan), and by December, they were acting directors.

By 1979, they became permanent directors, sharing total oversight of a 60 bed congregate facility and the 229 acre dairy farm. This involved caring for a 100-head Holstein herd, milking 50 Dairy cows, growing hay, feeding cows, growing vegetables and flowers, while working with 60 residents from ages 18 to 98 who contributed to all phases of the farm. They also trained several leader dogs for the blind and worked on 4-H projects with horses and even goats! The Collisons' three young children enjoyed family life together with residents, sharing meals to ballgames and concerts. Sara was the only licensed medical staff and was responsible for proper administration and training of staff.

When they first came to Ottawa County Community Haven, the residents were not part of the larger community. They rarely left the grounds to go anywhere. Dr. Dee Crittenden states humorously, "Well, you know Glen and Sara! They planned a few short trips to get their folks out into the world. With the first trip to the Sears Tower in Chicago, it took two hours to get the folks all loaded onto the bus. As the residents were coming in the front of the bus, others were exiting out. They were scared of the unknown, and the world was unknown to them."

As I later read this account in the 2007 SHALOM twentieth anniversary booklet, I could see how the Collisons' work at the Ottawa County Farm helped them transition to the nonprofit organization's current goals as well. I wondered how the Lord had led them to that farm and what moved them away?

Chapter 9 Challenge: God's name is *Jehovah Rophe*. The Lord who Heals Us. "Rophe can be translated to cure, cause to heal, physician or to make whole. It reveals that God is indeed the Great Physician, and the God who heals us" Exodus 15:26.

"If we are praying for a healing we would use the title *Jehovah-Rophe* or *Jehovah-Rapha*, the Lord God heals"(Psalm 147:3). God wants to heal not only our sicknesses and physical health but also our emotional health or even our "land" can be healed. "Rapha" means restoring something to its normal state.[1]

Have you transitioned from mere *belief* to complete *trust* in *Jehovah Rophe*?

---

[1]   Used by permission of Beth Rimstidt, www.child-bible-lessons.com

CHAPTER 10

The God of Provision in Transitions

D ecember 14, 2017 at the farm. When I drove up to Sara's cabin today, the farm was immersed in a blanket of fresh Michigan December snow. I had to agree that it was a bit hard at first to see the white alpaca in the snow, but there it was nestled by the gate, as if waiting for friends to come visit. The frosty snow scene reminded me of a metaphor I once heard which depicts forgiveness: *Snow* on a *Junkyard*!

Well, snow on a farm yard seems much the same. All the unseemly smelly parts of the farm are gently covered by pure white snow. I was thinking of this verse: Romans 5:8, "God demonstrated his love for us. While we were yet sinners [smelly junkyards] Christ died for us [covered us in robes of white washed in His blood sacrifice as a perfect Lamb, acceptable to God.]"

Sara can still look off her balcony to watch sheep, goats, chickens, rabbits, ducks, and alpaca all being cared for by the residents. Glen had a real vision for farm life here.

Looking back to the original 190 acres worked by Patrick Bunbury, God saw a mighty plan unfolding for the land. Interestingly, Bunbury was born in Ireland in 1806, so wouldn't he love to see all the sheep grazing on his former land with a Christian nonprofit organization redeeming back the purpose![1] Walking across the crunchy morning snow, I smiled about this.

So many major changes have come in just the last ten years (many illustrated by Sara and Glen's Christmas village collection that I got to see today). In 2014, a new maple sap evaporator was up and running! In 2015, they collected over 1000 gallons of sap to make twenty-five gallons of maple syrup from the trees on the SHALOM Farm. By 2013, SHALOM had built a new sugar shack.

Also in 2013, SHALOM Inc. began a work experience program with KRESA (Kalamazoo Regional Education Service Agency) with Parchment High School ASD (Autism Spectrum Disorder) class. Additionally, a full time WMU occupational therapy student internship was envisioned.

By 2014, SHALOM's four Nigerian dwarf goats, Suzy, Ruthie, Butterscotch, and Angel, made major public appearances.

Also in 2014, SHALOM residents helped hundreds of children and their families enjoy the goats at the Parchment Harvest Fest in October and the Christmas Wassailing in downtown Parchment (Michigan). The kids (the goats, that is) also participated in SHALOM's Living Nativity Worship on the farm!

The occupational therapy community service class at Western Michigan University built several playground structures for the goats.

---

[1] "1870 Cooper Township Census," Kalamazoo County, Kalamazoo, Michigan, http://www.fmschmitt.com/martin/stan/famtree/census/1870cooper3.htm

Grandpa Tiny's Farm, a petting farm in Frankenmuth, Michigan, gave the gift of Papa Tiny, our Nigerian dwarf buck.

In April of 2015, the farm was blessed with a gift of two alpacas! Grace was five years old, an experienced momma and eleven months pregnant! She gave birth to a baby alpaca (a cria) in June. Suki, a juvenile alpaca, was just ten months old. (She is all white in contrast to Grace's black.)

Eight lambs were also born that year, with more to follow to date!

More gifts came in the form of angora rabbits, Wilbur and Hope, and a Holland lop rabbit, Mikey.

Billy the fainting goat arrived and Sammy the LaMancha goat! Farm water and electric systems were installed. Chicks were delivered in September with new roofs on coops and a new mini-coop.

E.G.G.S. stands for Expressing God's Grace at SHALOM. Yes, they sell eggs.

Reading about all these additions to the farm, helped me appreciate the physical work but also the spiritual work going on behind the peaceful snowy farm scene.

Keith Lohman, executive director since 2007 tells us, "The SHALOM Farm is a place where adults and families living with disabilities can enjoy being close to the animals. This takes the form of helping with chores, walking and training sheep, goats, and alpaca, raising rabbits and showing them to visitors at the farm. We are building a real farm to serve real people, meeting real needs with real value."

In 2014, Keith Lohman noted that twenty chickens came to the cozy coop as a gift from our good friends of Bethesda Ranch AFC in Portage. Two chickens moved into the duck pen as a place of refuge from the others. Keith volunteered, "The ducks did not mind. Donated by a caring family, these two Peking ducks came with the names Mickey and Minnie. However, we now suspect they are both Mickey! We might change their names to Thanksgiving and Christmas since they had received invitations to dinner before finding refuge with SHALOM!"

As I walked up the long flight of stairs to the upper story, I could smell coffee and feel a warm fire. The scenery at Sara's cabin was indeed ready for the holidays. The table was lovingly set with freshly baked cookies and Grogg! I am still finding it hard to imagine that Sara's elegant home was once a twenty by forty cement block chicken coop. Then the creative addition came (twenty-five by forty foot) and went up a second floor.

Sara told me that tonight was the annual SHALOM holiday party—a big event. My family could not attend as we're packing up for a big trip to University of Illinois to attend our son Luke's doctoral graduation ceremony.

While we were enjoying coffee and a quiet morning, the phone rang. Sally, Sara's Bible study friend, had just lost her husband to cancer. We heard that she was singing the song "Silent Night" to him while he entered into Glory. Sara cried with her and began to share how God prepares us for these hard transitions, and I listened amazed to hear the spiritual strength forged from her own suffering when she lost Glen.

She spoke calmly, "I have walked this path. God will send you clarity and grace. Jeremiah 29:11 assures us that He knows the plans that He has for us, plans to prosper and not to harm us."

Tears flowed then she mentioned on the phone to Sally, "Leah Wendt is here. Do you need a pianist for the funeral?"

Instead of taking notes on the SHALOM story, I was handed the phone and began taking notes for sharing another beautiful life story. I listened to Sara's chimes playing peacefully from the fireplace mantel. I thought of how I had just experienced what she had told me about *Time*: God knows the road. He owns the map. Sara later told me, "Leah, I'm blessed to experience God's precious promise He gave me two days before He took my dearest home! I had asked how I was to complete my journey without my partner—the Lord's word says, 'My Presence will go with you, and I will give you rest.' [Exodus 33:14, NIV]—it's been true for six years! I'm grateful."

Looking at her Christmas village, I could see all the pieces that represented the amazing road map that God had led them to establish at the Homestead. I loved the sugar shack and candle dipping, Glen's hobbies. The Christmas tree farm was a special tribute to Glen's father who raised and sold Christmas trees. Well, I was also happy to add a new item to the massive scenes. I brought a little postman giving a package to a little girl. My husband, Roy, worked thirty-six years in the post office, so our community knows him well for being a faithful worker. Sara had a mailbox by a fence but no mailman! Ah, the "perfect place" in the village was waiting for my gift to come! I did not know about this empty place until I brought my gift, and suddenly, it was given an ideal spot, made *part of the family*, as if it had been waiting for years. This is how it feels to find SHALOM!

I love what C.S. Lewis says about heaven in his writings:

"Your soul has a curious shape because it is a hollow made to fit a particular swelling in the infinite contours of the divine substance, or a key to unlock one of the doors in the house with many mansions. For it is not humanity in the abstract that is to be saved, but you—you, the individual reader. Blessed and fortunate creature, your eyes shall behold Him and not another's. All that you are, sins apart, is destined, if you will let God have His good way, to utter satisfaction… Your place in Heaven will seem to be made for you, and you alone, because you were made for it."[2]

This is how many SHALOM volunteers, residents, and caregivers feel when they find peace and work in community together: God had a welcome mat waiting just for them, a perfect place prepared with a sense of belonging together in life.

Every current SHALOM newsletter praises the Lord for new volunteers. December 2017, they were so thankful that Pfizer employees came to work on landscaping, building a rabbit village, chicken coop, removing brush piles, and doing building repairs. Stryker volunteers came twice to care for fencing and roost and nesting boxes. Others came to serve at evening meals, worship, game nights, transportation to events, but more help is needed in so many areas! Kelly, the new 2017 SHALOM Woolery coach, is an occupational therapist who brings so many blessings to the residents. She drove by the Connection Depot thrift store sign for several years, but one day decided to go see what it was all about!

---

[2]   C. S. Lewis, *The Problem of Pain*, chapter 10, para. 3, 147–148.

Looking back at the Christmas village again, I smiled when I saw the "one-man-band" as I thought of Bert from the movie *Mary Poppins*. The greatest challenge of running a farm like SHALOM hinges on five areas which show this is not a one-man-band show.

1. *Volunteers* to provide social, spiritual, educational opportunities to residents. 2. *Focused work projects* for home maintenance. 3. *Donations* for home improvement, outreach, future development. 4. *Constant prayer* for caregivers, residents, and board members. 5. *Caring Community* to share the spiritual vision and ministry opportunities to live out the gospel and share *Shalom*.

How did God use the faith of two ordinary people to marshal such an army to serve so many in need? Isaiah 41:4 from the Living Bible explains it well: "Who has done such mighty deeds, directing the affairs of generations of mankind as they march by? It is I, the Lord, the First and Last. I alone am He!"

Before I left Sara's cabin that day, I came away with a deep sense of God's guiding hand, through many stormy trials in harsh Michigan winters. Sara had emphasized this before when telling me about her early years moving from Grand Rapids to Conklin, Michigan.

It was December of 1971, and Sara explained, "I was following Glen's U-Haul truck while driving our station wagon in a blizzard, with a vomiting child in the back seat!"

They would move to live above the grocery store, giving thanks for God's provision. Again, they answered the question, *What is in your hand?* Sara called those "hard days" where she could have allowed anger at God or bitterness to grow like a seed. Doing what you have to do will build maturity. In those days, Sara made her own baby food for their youngest child Julie and used cloth diapers!

Glen had been running a flower shop in the early years of their marriage, but people did not pay those bills on time. However, she admitted that this financial disaster in Allegan had tested their faith but led them to trust the Lord to move to Grand Rapids in September 1970. Glen was accepted into the Robert Hall Management Training Program during the month that their third child, Julie was born.

Sara also confided, "Glen and I always wanted a dozen kids. Instead, God always sent neighbor kids who needed us."

They had an opportunity to mentor an unwed mom and help a mom next door who had cancer. These trials would deepen their desire to do foster care.

So by 1971, they began searching for a home with a dream of doing foster care. They saw the empty grocery store in Conklin, Michigan and crunched the figures after overcoming their debts from the flower shop.

Sara replied, "By then, Glen was working at Robert Hall and an unwed pregnant teenager was placed with us by Bethany Christian Services. We provided her a home and a job—helping with babysitting. I decided that if I had to leave my three precious little ones to help other moms, I would pray for the best job possible."

That dream job came at the Kent County Health Department. Sara was hired as a public health nurse, doing holistic care but also as a visiting nurse around a heavy caseload with three school systems (two parochial and one public school) and the well-child clinic.

Sara continued to explain to me her struggle. Even though her work would increase her nursing skills to one day bless SHALOM, at this time (early 1970s) all she knew was that the *dream job* provided for the immediate financial need for their family. Every day with tears, she had to consciously surrender her will, not knowing what the future would hold. She had to surrender her rights and trust that God would fulfill his plans for the moment yet for the future. Sara would one day need professional nursing skills, administrative skills, and communication skills with government agencies and diverse groups within the community. Sara felt God knew that.

Finding the property in Conklin, however, suddenly made the dream of opening a foster home seem more real. A time of waiting followed. The home that drew them to Conklin was no longer available, but this vacant grocery store was. Apparently, the grocery store had been God's intention all along.

The grocery store offer came as a land contract with seventy dollars down. Glen had learned the grocery business working in his father's store on North Burdick, so he felt God was telling him to use *what was in his hand*. They were able to live above the store with their family and bring fresh food to their small Conklin community and participate in the volunteer fire department. They attended Conklin Reformed

Church and served as career staff for the Youth for Christ ministry, seeing revival and growth!

Glen had gleaned strong habits from his early store days with Lyle, his dad. In fact, Glen wrote in a family memory album, "I had my first job at age eleven, on Saturday mornings from 8 a.m. to 5 p.m. earning twenty-five cents per hour. I had to trim heads of lettuce, celery, and make bunches of bananas smaller. I also took care of empty bottles, and stacked cases, up to fifty cases! Later on, I moved up to cutting chicken, and the rest is history!"

Glen would go with his dad to watch him render lard for the grocery store. He also watched his dad cut meat and grind sausage. He also had many agricultural lessons taught to him from the farm life with his grandparents.

Using their small savings, the Collison Conklin Grocery Store opened in the spring of 1972 when God challenged them with this same thought: *What is in your hand?* Glen gave back to God what was in his hand. Every farm life, grocery store, and meat cutting skill from the past helped Glen rebuild their future. God had miraculously provided for this couple again! First Kings 17:11–14 also teaches us to just give to God what we have in our hand.

So he (Elijah) went to Zarephath. When he came to the town gate, a widow was there gathering sticks. He called to her and asked, "Would you bring me a little water in a jar so I may have a drink?" As she was going to get it, he called, "And bring me, please, a piece of bread."

"As surely as the LORD your God lives," she replied, "I don't have any bread—only a handful of flour in a jar and a little olive oil in a jug. I am gathering a few sticks to take home and make a meal for myself and my son, that we may eat it—and die."

Elijah said to her, "Don't be afraid. Go home and do as you have said. But first make a small loaf of bread for me from what you have and bring it to me, and then make something for yourself and your son. For this is what the LORD, the God of Israel, says: 'The jar of flour will not be used up and the jug of oil will not run dry until the day the LORD sends rain on the land.'"

Likewise, obedience would bring the Collisons this ample provision from 1971 to 1978. After hearing this story, I really wondered *what would God put in their hand next?*

Chapter 10 Challenge: Do you know this *Jehovah Jireh,* the Lord who provides? We cannot provide for our own salvation. Abraham named the place on the mountain *the Lord will provide* because at the right moment God provided a ram to sacrifice in place of his son Isaac.[3] Abraham trusted God in transition.[4]

Like the widow who needed food in the story in 1 Kings 17:11–14, you have to first give to God what you have, let go of what he asks for, before you will get what you need.

Are you willing to do that?

---

[3] Simcox, 17–18.

[4] Genesis 22, *Life Application Study Bible: New Living Translation.* (Wheaton, IL: Tyndale House Publishers, 1998), 23.

CHAPTER 11

A Taste of Home!

Thursday, January 11, 2018. When Sara and I met again for our coffee time chat after the New Year, Southwest Michigan was experiencing a sudden break in the subzero temperature pattern. With intensely warmer weather, we felt like we had been catapulted into spring break! As I drove up to the farm today, I saw SHALOM residents cheerfully feeding animals and doing morning chores in lighter jackets. The fifty-five degree temps had rolled in a heavy morning fog, and I felt transported to another climate! This unseasonal change would not be good for maple syrup, however. Sara observed that we need the deep cold of a winter season to keep the sap from running too soon, or *out of season*. (The sugar shack runs in March!)

The Apostle Paul offers this thought in 2 Timothy 4:2. The verse carries an interesting admonition telling us to preach the word *in season and out of season*. What an interesting verse to think about in January on a farm, where residents learn that everything from grape jellying to lambing or sheep shearing has its own season. While the fog on my pathway was *unseasonable* for January, it is never *untimely* or off season to sow seeds from the Word of God, especially on the spiritually *foggy days* when we need clearer vision! The Message version of the Bible states, "In simple humility, let our gardener, God, landscape you with the Word, making a salvation-garden of your life" (James 1:21). How amazing that our life can be like a garden all year long, *with no seasonal limitations!*

As to January, most of us are still using it to recover from December. Sara still had the snow village scenes gracing her cabin, and I felt happy to return to the "holiday season," if only just to go back in time and enjoy the peace (*shalom*) without the hectic scheduling part. Oddly, the spring-like weather made me feel like starting spring chores or fast forwarding past January. However, Sara's glowing fireplace still felt so welcoming! I sat down delightedly to Highlander Grogg, fudge, and cookies nestled on Christmas plates. We need Januarys.

Sara asked me, "How did your granddaughter like the decorated sugar cookie which I sent home with you last time?"

I reported back, "Well, her response was a bit enlightening. I told her that the cookie was from my friend Mrs. Collison who loves Jesus, but she replied, 'Really, Nana, and she loves us too? Doesn't she know we have some issues over here?'"

I told her, "Well, yes, she knows about that (autism), but she still loves us because God still loves us."

Sara replied, "Oh, Leah, this is the very heart of SHALOM. We are all disabled. We all need Jesus. These precious residents can and are being discipled in homes with a family. The home is God's ordained unit."

Then I relayed to Sara, "When I asked our granddaughter if she liked the sugar cookie, her eyes grew wide and she exclaimed, 'Oh yes, Nana! This is so good—it is God's Turkish Delight!'"

God's Turkish delight was a new concept for sure. However, we had been reading aloud C.S. Lewis's book *The Lion, The Witch, and The Wardrobe*. Like the old Testament character, Esau who gave up his family inheritance (birthright) for one taste of lentil soup, Lewis's character Edmund was led astray by one taste of Turkish delight. This tempting treat came from the White Witch who made everything like *Winter in Michigan* but without Christmas!

I tried to imagine God offering a heavenly version of Turkish delight that would tempt us *like the joy of Christmas, as refreshing as spring air in the dead of winter!* One taste of this would be so sweet we would follow and never refuse his wishes! C.S. Lewis explains just such a taste of something heavenly, which he called "joy" in his biography *Surprised by Joy*.

Well, little granddaughter and I had purchased Turkish delight just to try it; rose flavored tasted like you were eating perfume or chewing soap with a very strong rose oil smell. There are few things comparable to the texture in a western diet. We did not try pistachio or ginger flavors! Ancient legend states that a sultan once summoned all his expert confectioners to a competition to create a rare expensive dessert to help him cope with his harem full of wives! Turkish delight was born out of this high stress family challenge![1]

I agreed with Sara that chocolate was invented just to help us cope with winter, and her minty fudge this morning was wonderful. However, I also agreed that for many of the adult residents with developmental disabilities, this new taste of home at SHALOM offers a newfound independence with joy.

The story of the third home (1990—Homestead North) has a Michigan pioneer background. Sara told me that this third home

with three names (called Homestead North, then Respite House but now SHALOM Three Pines) came to them in the most unique way. Their friend Dave, the father of a Homestead resident, was a realtor. He had stopped by the Homestead one day but suddenly had car trouble and needed a jumpstart. Glen went out to help him, and in the course of that encounter, he heard that an amazing property was for sale across the street! What a great blessing to acquire a third home, Homestead North!

Rob and Chris McGuire first opened the home, and then Dan and Holly Collison became the adult foster care providers there from 1991–1996 and cared for six men, then sold the home to Dan and Crystal Dexter in 1996. The Dexters and their four children Evan, Seth, Luke and Grace enjoyed living together as an extended family with the residents. They also took good care of this historic brick home until SHALOM Inc. as a 501(c) (3) nonprofit organization was able to purchase it in 1999, with the encouragement of our newest board member June Taft.

---

[1] "Turkish Delight Legend," http://www.sultans.co.uk/history.htm

Apparently, Philo Vrandenburg, a native of Dutchess County, New York, "came to Michigan in 1833 and bought the farm on the River Road [6276 Riverview Drive]."[2] He and his wife Alice *cleared the land* and for a time, even housed the ex-governor of New York, Enos Throop, a relative and a widower. Throop needed shelter while building his home on Springbrook farm. That phrase *cleared the land,* implies great perseverance and hard labor! Glen would love this.

The farm was enlarged after 1869 when Philo's daughter Emily and son-in-law Clarence Vanderbuilt built the large brick house (SHALOM Three Pines). In 1925, after changing ownership several times, the home was purchased by Sterling and Elizabeth Welborn whose son Robert served in the house of representatives and Jack who served as a Michigan senator.[3] This home housed men of character!

Deanna Smith was the care provider when the brick home was first named the SHALOM Respite House, offering short term care for residents of the community, over a weekend or up to ten days at a time. Then in 2003, this Respite House was changed to a group home and renamed SHALOM Three Pines, an adult foster care facility for women. Karen and Don Rome and children Zach and Ellie came to live there in 2006.

---

2   Christlieb, 92.
3   Ibid.

How did Sara learn so much about the home's history? One day, she and Glen were painting window trim at the newly purchased home [Three Pines] when a car pulled into the driveway. A couple came with their ninety-year old mother who was taking a sentimental journey from Kentucky to Michigan to visit her old family farm! The 90-year-old great granddaughter of Philo Vrandenburg (Althea Virgina Allen) had pictures from 1896, complete with horse and buggy parked nearby, and Clarence and Emily Vanderbuilt were in the photo! Philo Vrandenburg was a *commissioner of highways* in Kalamazoo in 1871, '74, '76, and '78. He died in 1888. Wouldn't he be amazed to see his home in 2018 with our modern roads![4]

Prior to SHALOM's ownership, the home had been divided into three apartments, so Althea was thrilled to hear that it was again one home for a family. Althea gave Sara a real taste of the home's past. She was delighted to see inside and share how each room was used in the late 1800s. Modern owners removed the cupola, the brick oven, and made an efficiency apartment in the woodshed area behind the kitchen. Most of us do not relate to the concept of a *winter kitchen* cook stove to warm the house but a *summer kitchen* on a porch or an outdoor brick oven to keep a home cooler. Local Parchment school children observe this Michigan pioneer history at the Delano Homestead, built nearby in 1858.[5]

I was amazed by the beauty of this stately brick home. Even more amazing was the next goal for SHALOM: to build only as God provides and remain debt free. They also dictated that these homes be biblical and Christ-centered to love those in their care. The board of directors believing God for the impossible, set a goal of four homes to be developed in ten years. The three existing Homesteads were to be the model with shared values and goals.

As Glen said about the ministry, "God provided knowledgeable, skilled, and willing people to serve on a board: Sally Lindsay, Sara Collison, Tom Lowing, Daniel Collison, Noreen Jolliffe, John Westra, Mark Pulver and Attorney Garry Walton, while Bruce Lenardson came shortly after the first board meeting held October 16, 1990." By 1993, the SHALOM board started building the home on Polk street. Glen wrote, "Through the committed efforts of Harry and Edna Meier and

---

4   "Kalamazoo Township History," http://genealogytrails.com/mich/kalamazoo/kalamazootwp.html
5   See "Kalamazoo Nature Center," https://naturecenter.org/Locations/DeLano-Farms

Tom and Shirley Hill and God's army of volunteers [Mobile Missionary Assistance Program] and many generous donors, SHALOM was ready to build their first home."

Board member and architect Tom Lowing designed the Polk Street home, which was ready to serve SHALOM residents by June 1995. Board member and Contractor Mark Pulver oversaw the project. Leo Nyhof came to work with his "halo" from a broken neck. He and other dedicated volunteers of Haven Church worked alongside Brad Stonerock. Jack and Erin Hoogendyk, along with their children Jacob, Isaiah, Maria, Caitlin, and Benjamin, moved in and painted and proudly opened the SHALOM Polk street home, a community labor of love to make a home.

Jack has always been "a voice of reason and a champion for special needs people in Michigan" as Dr. Dee Crittenden has called him. Jack Hoogendyk who went on to serve with the Michigan House of Representatives (2003–2008, 61st district) was also honored by the Michigan Assisted Living Association in 2006 for his work on behalf of Michigan citizens with developmental disabilities.

Tom and Julie Hermenitt would follow the Hoogendyks as Polk Street Care Providers in 1996 along with their children Rebekah and Zachery. Tom was recognized by the Michigan Assisted Living Association in 2007 for leadership in home management and was awarded one of five "Spirit of Service Awards" given in the state (Sara and Glen would win this award in 2009). Tom remembers the day he was called and asked to join SHALOM as care providers. Feeling the call from God, they made SHALOM Polk Street AFC their home, ministry and their life, serving adult men with developmental disabilities. Tom compares his experience with Moses, who also "received a call and obeyed, not knowing what he was getting into."

Reading that comment by Tom, I realized that he too had followed Glen's passion to answer the very same question: *What is in your hand?*

In 1994, a home on Van Buren Street across from the SHALOM Polk Street Home (then under construction) was donated by Roger Niebor's family. Roger had support from Gary and Lana Thompson and then Deanna Smith, on his quest for self-determination and supported independence. Pastor Keith Lohman wrote this tribute, 2014:

Roger had gumption! In spite of major limitations due to cerebral palsy, Roger lived a full life. He would wash the siding on his house as high as he could reach, then ask someone to do the upper part. He would snow blow his own driveway. After all, he had to get his car out to get the mail and groceries. Roger kept his own house, vacuuming and cooking and doing his own laundry. He even decorated for Christmas with a giant, lighted snowman out front. Roger always had the gumption to do for himself. Roger was thoughtful. One time, a storm caused several large tree branches to fall in his back yard. So a couple of guys were helping Roger clean up the larger branches. It was a really hot and humid summer day. After helping and directing for a while, Roger mysteriously disappeared inside. After a little time, out he came with large glasses of ice cold lemonade!

Roger was thankful. Whenever someone helped with a repair or errand or whatever it was, he always said "thank you." I was always touched by this. This man, with severe limitations, was thankful. I was always humbled by his absolute sincerity of gratitude. He knew he needed help, and somehow he knew I needed to help! He was thankful.

From Roger I learned interdependence. He was not hesitant to ask for help as I might be. Yet he would not allow others to do what he could do for himself. It was never hard to get a phone call to go help Roger because he never played the victim. He did not take advantage of those who helped. Somehow he made me feel privileged to be asked into his life. I needed him too.

I asked Roger more than once about his relationship with Jesus. Although he could not talk clearly, and communication was always a challenge, it was very clear that Roger believed in Jesus as his Savior. As he acknowledged Jesus's forgiveness of his sins, Jesus's death on a cross and resurrection, I told him more than once that this made us brothers in Christ!

That we are brothers in Christ is a declaration like no other. Here we stand before the cross, equally needy and equally blessed in the riches of Christ!

We will catch up to you soon, Brother. We love you, Roger, and miss you!

That is such a beautiful testimony to write about Roger. The more I talk to Sara, and hear these stories, the more I realize that she and Glen were pioneers in adult foster care homelife. In 2006, their daughter Julie's work with adults with disabilities was noted by the Michigan Assisted Living Association, and she was awarded one of five Spirit of Services Awards in Michigan for leadership in home management. As Glen contended, "Sharing life together in a family gave meaning and purpose for everyone."

Sara remarked that most of her spiritual journey into *shalom* has been just like this too, "Leah, we either get to listen to God when he says *trust me*, or we get to be angry and frustrated trying to figure out life on our own."

As Tom Hermenitt described their *shalom* path to obedience as adult care providers from 1996 to 2016, "The job was living life every day with people who needed me. People would say *you are really special doing that*. But I would answer, 'No, we heard God's call and know this is our call to obey.'"

As I left the farm today, I began to see how the gift of a home teaches SHALOM residents how God, "our help in ages past" is still our "hope for years to come. Our shelter from the stormy blast, and our *eternal home.*"[6]

Chapter 11 Challenge: His name is *Jehovah Shammah*, God is There/Present.[7] "Appearing only once in Scripture, this name fortifies the concept of God's omnipresence. He has been and always shall be there, or present. There has never been a time or a situation where He has not been." Reach out to the God who wants to claim you in His family and make His home in your heart. Revelations 3:20 affirms, "Here I am! I stand at the door and knock. If anyone hears my voice and opens the door, I will come in and eat with that person [*fellowship together around the table of life*], and they with me."

6 Isaac Watts, *Our God, Our Help in Ages Past,* 1719.
7 Simcox, 17–18.

Living with an Open Hand

So many of the SHALOM Inc. staff and volunteers know how much Sara misses Glen, especially every January, but she calmly confirmed, "Leah, this last step was again about full submission and obedience. You have to hear how God led me to do this in His Love. You have to keep your relationships on the palm of your open hand." Again I could not wait to hear this story. She talked about that summer,

"I was visiting our kids Dan and Holly in Minnesota in August 2012. While having my quiet time on their balcony, I was talking to the Lord about all the changes I was now facing. The thought just came to me after prayer that I should melt our wedding rings into a single piece of jewelry. Little thoughts are like seeds planted by the Holy Spirit. He is planting something beautiful if only we will listen. I felt that about the ring idea."

"My daughter-in-law Holly suggested to me, 'Let's go shopping. We need to find something wedding worthy to attend the wedding in New York.'"

"You see Glen had told our niece a year ago, 'you set the date, and we will be there'. I did not want to miss it since Glen had been such an *encourager* to her. Well, Holly and I found the most elegant teal formal evening jacket, and I already had a nice skirt to match it. The problem was that empty neckline really needed a stunning necklace to complete the formal look."

Sara felt very encouraged to take this next step to design a single jewelry piece composed of their wedding rings. Her daughter Julie (Kortz) Stevens also had a wedding ring from Glen's mother while Sara had a special gold valentine's day heart from Glen. Sara had Glen's wedding band plus his fortieth anniversary wedding band.

She was ready to add her ring too, but confessed honestly, "You wonder if the timing is right to make big decisions. Julie expressed her support agreeing that the wedding was great timing to have the piece created, since that would feel like Glen was with me in spirit at this big family event. Leah, are we ever ready to give up our plans for God's perfect timing? You see, we must live with an open hand of surrender."

"I want the next generation to know that God drew us together to be life partners. He knows best what He has designed us to do. I was always the finisher, never jumping into a new project until one was done. Whereas, Glen was the adventurous seeker, knocking on new doors, trying unexplored things, seeing what is possible. Many couples live in a happy ever after delusion, but hard work can unite you together when you trust your partner. God united us so uniquely that quitting on Him now would be disobedience, denying His plan. God had orchestrated it all."

On that last week of August 2012 in Minnesota, her family took her to the state fair. How that reminded her of the first dates to the local Michigan fairs with Glen in the fall of 1964. She was also remembering their fortieth anniversary weekend (2005) which was in Minnesota with a renewal of their vows. Was she really now ready to take the rings to Nord's Jewelers?

Glen's ring was taken off him right away when he fell ill and was at the University of Michigan Hospital in January 2012. She remembers things in a bit of a fog now, but the doctor had it taken off due to swelling. Then Glen's ring was on a chain which she just wore around her neck for a long time.

The fortieth anniversary band carried a happier memory of renewing their vows at a ceremony in Minnesota. Their family had surprised them with a CD copy of their original vows taken off a reel to reel tape recorder at Anchor Point. Sara remembered, "It was so wonderful to have the fortieth anniversary. I wasn't sure Glen would go for the idea of re-saying the vows, but he agreed. This generation needs to see a visible example of committed love. As for melting the rings into one piece of jewelry, I really felt that I was supposed to do it."

With that firm decision, she contacted a jeweler and asked what could be done in two weeks, to have it ready to wear for that wedding in New York! This beautiful piece of jewelry was to be the symbol of the unity and beauty forged through suffering.

The day she had planned to take the rings to the jeweler, she arrived there only to realize that she could not find the rings. Thinking she had just left them at home on the table, she went back home. Nothing was on the table. She searched and searched in an intense effort, but no results.

Next, she called her good friend Esther, "the prayer warrior for lost things." Sara asked her to pray. The loss of the rings was troubling to her. Somewhere was a plastic bag with five precious rings.

After the prayers went out late that night, she was looking in her car and noticed a tiny corner of plastic, which she thought nothing about at first. Suddenly, she felt the urge to look one more time, and there deeply sandwiched under the passenger's seat, she pulled out the missing plastic bag with their rings. What was accomplished in this extra day of waiting? Sara advised calmly, "With that one extra day of hunting for the rings, I had come to the SHALOM farm team morning meeting realizing that I had yet to climb Mount Moriah. During the prayer time at the beginning while others prayed, God reminded me of Abraham's journey up the mountain to surrender his son—a feat of faith and obedience."

What did she mean? As Abraham was asked to give up Isaac to test his faith in God's plan, she had to give Glen back to God. In Genesis 22, Abraham confirms his faith during this strange test: God wanted to know just how much Abraham trusted in him to provide, *Jehovah Jireh*. A song by Michael Card offers the dramatic moment:

A rush of wind and an angel's voice, A ram in the thicket caught by his horns, And a new age of trusting the Lord is born
For God has provided a Lamb, He was offered up in your place
What Abraham was asked to do he has done, He's offered his only son.[1]

---

[1] Michael J Card, *God Will Provide a Lamb*, eLYRICS, (Benson Records, 1993), https://www.elyrics.net/read/m/michael-card-lyrics/god-will-provide-a-lamb-lyrics.html.

When Sara first dated Glen, the challenge was the same. She told me that she had to give him back to God emotionally. Now once again, she must give him back to God, even though she had already given him up physically.

What Jeff from Nord Jeweler's had in mind expressed this vivid picture of her altar sacrifice. She felt the Lord say, "Give Glen to me." The jeweler used part of the wedding band with its rubies and diamonds to make the bail that holds the circular pendant. The birthstones of their children are embedded in this circular pendant of hammered gold. The diamond from Sara's engagement ring is set central in the circle, like a focal point on the pendant. This circular symbol of eternity, forged through fire and water in a Japanese process of hammered gold, represents a symbolic new beginning to Sara. She proposed, "You see I am still bonded tightly in a love relationship."

The Jewelers suspended Sara's gold valentine heart freely in the middle. Her reaction of surprise rewarded their creative efforts. She had no idea how stunning the final result would be. I can see how trust went into the whole process of letting go in order to make something new.

Sara confirms, "This dynamic piece represents my new creation, my new beginning, my mission that I must fulfill. Writing this book has been on my heart, along with seeing that SHALOM Inc. would continue to grow. In Luke 9:23–24, Jesus said to them all 'Whoever wants to be my disciple must deny themselves and take up their cross daily and follow me.[24] For whoever wants to save their life will lose it, but whoever loses their life for me will save it.'" If we open our hand, God will fill it with his plan.

Chapter 12 Challenge: God's name is *Jehovah Nissi*. The word *Nissi* is "Hebrew for standard, ensign, banner or flag. These items were often taken into battle and used as rallying points for troops as they engaged the enemy.[2]

What is in your hand that you must let go before you can accept the *Jehovah Nissi's* battle plan for your life?

---

2 Simcox, 17–18.

CHAPTER 13

The Lord Is My Shepherd/Warrior

January 24, 2018. When I drove down snowy Riverview Drive today, I was still pondering all the grueling national news of the last few weeks. My precious former piano student, Rachael DenHollander had just given her victim statement in a Lansing courtroom. She asserts that she only spoke up against her abuser for one reason: obedience. In an interview with *Christianity Today*, Rachael reaffirmed, "He [Jesus Christ] needs your obedience. Obedience means that you pursue justice, and you stand up for the oppressed, and you stand up for the victimized."[1]

While calling for the maximum penalty, she still showed grace to her accuser:

> "The Bible you speak of carries a final judgment where all of God's wrath and eternal terror is poured out on men like you. Should you ever reach the point of truly facing what you have done, the guilt will be crushing. And that is what makes the gospel of Christ so sweet. Because it extends grace and hope and mercy where none should be found. And it will be there for you.

---

[1] Morgan Lee, "My Larry Nassar Testimony Went Viral: But There's More to the Gospel Than Forgiveness," last updated January 31, 2018, http://www.christianitytoday.com/ct/2018/january-web-only/rachael-denhollander-larry-nassar-forgiveness-gospel.html

I pray you experience the soul crushing weight of guilt so you may someday experience true repentance and true forgiveness from God, which you need far more than forgiveness from me—though I extend that to you as well."[2]

Rachael's words of truth left the audience shocked and stunned with many wrestling over her choice to obey a God who is both truthful and merciful like this. I have only to look at the oxymoron of a *peaceful fire* in Sara's stone fireplace to visualize the same recondite mystery. Fire cooks food or warms us but sterilizes and destroys. God's character qualities seem as inseparable as those of fire. I too was wrestling with the mystery as I prayed for her on the way to the farm. Stand up for truth out of obedience: Yes, for the precious ones they serve, this was the same call on Glen and Sara's lives, and on the SHALOM caregivers.

As I ascended the cabin stairs today, Sara had big news. Another blessing is now in the hand of SHALOM! Giant sheets of building blueprints graced the dining room table. We laid our hands on a half-million-dollar plan and prayed for God to use and protect a new SHALOM Woolery building. As I flipped through the pages and sipped Grogg with cream, I could hardly imagine how excited Glen would have been. In 2012, after he passed away, his vision was taking shape: using farm life to prepare residents for meaningful work.

There was an added blessing, however, which Glen had prayed to come to fruition. (Sara said he always loved to pray in the garden with a hoe in hand!) Pastor Keith Lohman writes, "The SHALOM Woolery's purpose is growth in wholeness through Jesus Christ, mentally, emotionally, physically, and relationally, in the context of meaningful work, through a coop-

---

2   Rachael DenHollander, "Read Rachel DenHollander's Full Impact Statement About Larry Nassar," CNN, updated January 30, 2018, https://www.cnn.com/2018/01/24/us/rachael-denhollander-full-statement/index.html

erative team approach. The SHALOM Inc. Woolery was established in 2012, offering adults living with developmental, intellectual, emotional, and physical disabilities a safe place to learn and practice a productive lifestyle. The SHALOM Woolery currently operates in the SHALOM Shepherd's Barn, where our activity center, office and thrift store are also located. Due to growth, vision, and need, we are seeking more dedicated space for people, work activities, inventory, supplies, looms, washing and work tables. SHALOM'S newest building [2018] will be the future home of our ongoing SHALOM Woolery Ministry, at the corner of Riverview and Van Buren street in the sheep pasture. Plans for a 3000 square foot building [two levels with balcony] are nearly complete. The SHALOM Woolery campus will include the Pavilion, a future sheep barn, a green pasture, and a pond of quiet waters [to reflect the message in Psalm 23.]"

Sara exclaimed they were all rather excited about finding the natural spring, which means a pond can enter the blueprints. I looked at the pages and pages of blueprint designs rather in awe of it all myself. *He leadeth me beside still waters* (Psalm 23). That scene is going to be so beautiful! There is an old version of the shepherd Psalm that I love by Isaac Watts, also the composer of *Joy to the World.* "The sure provisions of my God attend me all my days. O may Your House be my abode, and all my work be praise. There would I find a settled rest, while others go and come; no more a stranger, or a guest, but like a child at home."[3]

Holly Collison wrote about this same feeling in her tribute letter to Glen and Sara, presented at an anniversary banquet in 2007. She tells how she felt *at home in the fold*:

"I have since been reflecting on the first time I met my in-laws. We all either romanticize or diminish our past experiences. I recognize this. But for me, without exaggeration, meeting my soon to be husband's parents was pure magic. Seeing the Homesteads for the first time was a moment of eureka for my young, newly embraced, Christian faith. Here were believers living out their faith in service to the most needy of society—the developmentally disabled. They strove to healthfully and skillfully draw from the Homestead land as much as possible and included the residents in the work. I loved my in-laws immediately. In fact, I will venture to say that

---

3   Isaac Watts, *My Shepherd Will Supply My Need*, 1719.

though I was already in love with their son, their life of serving Jesus by proxy of others and their earthiness was influential in sealing the deal.

"After marrying and having moved our life to Michigan to join them in the work, my understanding of them grew in stature and appreciation... In true homage to her [my own mom's] training, I excelled at organizing my household even with the addition of six men living with us and possessing varying degrees of disability. As a bonus to my life, Mom and Dad Collison additionally taught me a myriad of homegrown activities. With them, I learned to organically garden, boil wool, tap trees and make maple syrup, can fruits and vegetables, make homemade candy and bargain shop. I accidentally burned it [maple syrup] into sugar candy once and was in tears. Dad Collison said, 'Bah, just add water again! It worked!' I learned to make homemade bread and still have the recipe memorized. Long before there was a Sam's Club or Costco, we were running down to Indiana Amish Co-ops for bulk cinnamon and cream of tartar. I learned to sew and to pile black walnuts on the two tracks of the driveway and drive over them to make shucking easier for Grandpa.

"One day, Dad Collison brought over a brand-new cheese mold with a recipe instruction book, just for me. Today, at this point in my life, it makes me chuckle to think of the absurdity of someone such as me learning to make cheese. But at the point in my history, living on the Homestead, it was as natural as getting up each morning. Gallons and gallons of milk were needed to make one decent sized wheel of cheese.

"Bo-Bonnie, our one Jersey cow, happily provided milk. I learned to let the milk curdle with the rennet for just the right amount of time—to heat the curd exactly according to the recipe, and to press, and press, and press, and press some more. I discovered paraffin's true use, whose function preceded by centuries its use as an ingredient of a luxury pedicure! Who knew? Day after day, I went out to the barn refrigerator to turn the cheese as it aged. Cheeses in all their different forms, contain essentially the same ingredients. The differences really boil down to five distinctions: the type of milk, the level of heat used, amount of water/whey extracted, the amount of salt added, and aging. Rennet makes it congeal.

"One day, near Christmas, I went to do my daily flipping of the cheese but the wheels were gone. I high-tailed it over to Mom and Dad Collison's house, and I found them sitting at the kitchen table, neatly wrapping triangles of cheese in pretty paper to give to us as gifts. I had worked so hard to make that cheese, and I thought that I should have the distinction of deciding how it was used. I roared like a lion.

"Interrupting me, Dad Collison said, 'Whatever is said here, is said in love because we are family.' He didn't point his finger at me, but rather his whole hand. Herein is the spice of living together in a small community and as a family.

"Perhaps making cheese is an appropriate metaphor for how I spent my twenties. Whole milk *love*, gallons and gallons of it needed to pro-cure a full-bodied cheese makes a strong family. Rennet is like the adult residents, a [natural complex] enzyme is needed to set up the cheese and comes from an [indispensable] external source. Cheese would not be cheese without rennet; it causes us to work together to refine our rela-tionships [changing the whole destiny of the final product.]

"Careful heating and measuring of salt as balance defines the type of cheese; this balance causes our individual personalities [like different types of cheese] to shine. The press work and the trials that are embodied in it squeezes the whey and water out; this refines our love for Jesus and our understanding of being His hands and feet in the world today. Paraffin covering provides protection from molds and damage, protects the treasure of each other!

"I have personally witnessed the fact that for others to even consider Christianity an option, they have needed to see the way that I am differ-ent because of faith. I learned how to roar like a lion while treating those around me with respect and loving kindness. I learned to take radical risks."

In her tribute, Holly Collison further tells how they peppered the family gatherings with laughter and old memories. Holly offered one word of comical advice, "Never, never, never transport a small calf in a minivan! Eww..." I would love to hear more on that story someday. There are so many funny farm photos!

Holly mentioned taking *radical risks*. Sara said that once even their tax man thought they were a bit out of their minds to accept the call to do foster care as God sent them to do. Yet they stepped out in faith, since they knew that victory belongs to *Jehovah Sabaoth*, the God of hosts of angel armies.[4]

Next week, Feb. 10–17, 2018, another team is stepping out on faith to help abused women: Phil Vlietstra (SHALOM board president) Andie and Keith Lohman (SHALOM's executive director and his wife), Cindy Luyendyk, Denise Ericks, Grace Demi, Kim Dickens, Margaret and Larry VanderPlas and Lin Batts will be going to Guatemala on a service team. The group will support Grace Demi's grandson, Brian Reynolds, who works with Kids Alive International to rescue at-risk young women. They will be doing construction/maintenance, teaching English as a second language, and working in the orphanage, along with whatever else God has in store. SHALOM supporters prayed for them to be God's conduits of love, as we know that they will be serving at Oasis, which actively engages a culture that is filled with victims of sexual and physical abuse.

Pastor Lohman taught in our Haven Church Bible study this Sunday that the Hebrew word for justice is "mishpat," occurring more than 200 times in the Old Testament. He gave the class an article by Tim Keller who adds, "Realize, then, how significant it is that the biblical writers introduce God as a father to the fatherless, a defender of widows [Psalm 68:4–5]."[5] I saw that same verse on the Kids Alive website with a page for San Lucas, Guatemala.[6]

This week, I was also in prayer with more volunteers. I was invited by Sara to attend the SHALOM worship at the Shepherd's Barn (held the first Saturday of the month at 6:30 p.m.) As residents spoke about their burdens, I saw the joy of a family keeping bonds of trust with the honor of guarding their safe place. I heard stories of hearts learning to give their chains to Christ and walk in freedom. I also left with the joyful feeling of being like a "child at home," not like a "stranger or a guest" to the fold.[7]

As for Rachael DenHollander and her family, this tumultuous week has had a resolute ending like in Exodus 15:3: "The LORD is a

---

4 Simcox, 17–18.

5 Tim Keller, Minister at Redeemer Presbyterian Church in New Your City asks the question, "What is Biblical Justice?" Relevant, https://relevantmagazine.com/god/practical-faith/what-biblical-justice

6 Guatemala, "Kids Alive International," 2018, https://www.kidsalive.org/where-we-work/country-66/

7 Isaac Watts, *My Shepherd Will Supply My Need*, 1719.

warrior; Yahweh is his name!" Are we teaching the world that Jesus is the Shepherd Warrior?

Rachael's parents celebrated their thirty-seventh wedding anniversary in a courtroom in Lansing listening to their daughter give a speech that rocked social media. I had joined the army of prayer warriors. I had played the piano for Rachael and Jacob's wedding (2009), so hearing she is expecting their fourth child made me so thankful. She and Jacob will be joyfully rocking babies to Michael Card: "My [child], life's a battle, so you be a rebel [warrior]. Stand ready to fight. And never stop loving the light [follow the Shepherd]."[8]

As I left the farm today, I was surely hoping we could record all these stories of journeys toward *shalom*, journeys toward victory and healing, stories from North America to Central America. We may need a second book (or as Pastor Craig Gilbert from Haven Church taught us, Heaven will be full of stories that have not been written down! Just imagine hearing them all. John 20:30–31, Jesus performed many other signs in the presence of his disciples, which are not recorded in this book. But these are written that you may believe that Jesus is the Messiah, the Son of God, and that by believing you may have life in his name.)

One final challenge came out of this week's notes: Rachel DenHollander asked the world, "How much is a little girl worth?"

Years ago, I was shopping with our autistic granddaughter when she pleaded with the clerk to "pleeease" use the handheld scanner to price check her little hand. The clerk looked confused, but I encouraged her to show her how it worked. The clerk scanned her small hand and showed her the big row of *zeroes*! But to the clerk's amazement, our little granddaughter chirped out happily, "Yes. That is right. I am *priceless*. No price on me!"

God has often demonstrated to SHALOM how He loves and values people. In early spring 2011, the SHALOM executive director received a call from a Christian nonprofit organization that cared for unwed pregnant women. They were getting ready to sell a property near the SHALOM Network and wondered if we would be interested in expanding its outreach. After one look at the property, our board unanimously agreed that God was asking us to take this step of faith. Within just a few months, God had prepared and called a very special couple, Brian and Kathy Herminett and supernaturally funded the project.

---

[8]   Michael Card, *Nathan's Song*, Youtube, Sparrow Records, 1993, https://www.youtube.com/watch?v=zsr_VYRzk7Q

Astounded, Keith Lohman our executive director said, "God must have something really important for this home!"

The plan quickly became evident when SHALOM Growing Grace home welcomed its first resident who was a deaf, eighteen-year-old whose mother had recently passed away. This young man found Christ as his Lord and Savior and his loving, new caregiver mom Kathy, taught herself sign language to be able to communicate with him! The journey of grace had begun for this young man and for others that soon joined this precious family. The value of a deaf young man and a couple open and obedient to the call of God—priceless!

Chapter 13 Challenge: "God is *Jehovah Sabaoth. Tzavoat* is the Hebrew word that becomes *Sabaoth* in the English Bible. It speaks of a mass, throng, or host of persons organized for or waiting for war or those who have assembled for war. In Israel today, the word is well-known as a part of the name of the Israel Defense Forces (IDF) *Tzava Ha haganah L'Yisrael,* which literally means the host or army for the protection of Israel or the Lord of the armies of Heaven."[9]

---

[9] Simcox, 17–18.

Are you safe and at home in His Sheepfold or are you still a stranger and a guest to his loving offer? Charles Hadley Spurgeon writes, "The cry of the Christian faith is the gentle word, *Come*. The law was a dispensation of terror, which drove men before it as with a scourge. The gospel draws with bands of love. Jesus is the Good Shepherd going before His sheep, bidding them follow Him, and ever leading them onwards with one sweet word, *Come!*"[10]

---

[10] Charles Hadley Spurgeon, *Morning by Morning* (Grand Rapids, MI: Baker Book House, 1975), 351.

CHAPTER 14

"I'll Fly Away"

Glen Collison was born October 17, 1941 in Kalamazoo, the son of Lyle and Ruth (Pike) Collison. On August 26, 1965, he was united in marriage to the former Sara L. Goldstein. Glen spent himself on behalf of others.

February 2012, Dave Person, freelance writer for the Kalamazoo Gazett noted in a tribute to Glen:

As members of Haven church sang Christmas carols in the hallways of Borgess Gardens, Glen Collison strolled along behind, one hand moving up and down the keyboard of his accordion, the other hand squeezing the bellows. The carols brought several residents of the nursing home to their doors, many with smiles lighting up their faces, others listening intently or singing along, as Collison continued his accompaniment, ignoring the fifty-pound weight of the instrument on his shoulders. After the festivities, Glen Collison and his wife, Sara, who had been playing her violin, were putting away their instruments when they were approached by a family member of a resident who had one last request of the pair. Out came the instruments again and within minutes the Collisons were in his room playing "I'll Fly Away," a fast-paced, uplifting hymn: Some glad morning when this life is over, I'll fly away.

Dave Person notes, "It was a snapshot of the way Glen Collison lived his life, always in service to others."

A few weeks later, in early January, Collison, 70, became ill, and on Jan. 14, 2012, a day after the illness was diagnosed as acute leukemia, he died. Humble, yet strong in his Christian faith, according to his family and friends, Collison made it a practice to go out of his way to encourage and care for people from all walks of life. Foremost among them were people with developmental disabilities, dozens of whom he and his wife had shared their homes and lives with. Collison enjoyed teaching and led adult and children's Sunday school classes and a midweek Bible study; introduced children to life on his SHALOM farm where he raised sheep, goats, chickens, and ducks, tapped maple trees in the spring and pressed apples into cider each fall; and shared his skills on the accordion with others who wanted to learn to play the instrument.

He paid attention to people, who to the rest of the world, wouldn't matter, and he made them feel that they mattered. "He impacted so many lives," agreed the Rev. Keith Lohman, a pastor teaching at Haven Church (Kalamazoo) and also current executive director of SHALOM Inc., this ministry founded by the Collisons that provides care for people with developmental disabilities. "God put a fire in his heart to love and serve people," recalls Sara Collison.

Sara and Glen's granddaughter Alyssa, in her mid-twenties, is now a coach at SHALOM. She also saw that quality in her grandfather.

Granddaughter Alyssa recalls, "I treasure the work I did with Grandpa Collison on the farm each summer, growing up, milking goats, feeding and caring for the animals, making goat soap and goat cheese. The irony is that I often stayed in the farm cabin which is now transformed into our farm ready room. I loved asking Grandpa questions and soaking up his knowledge of farm life. I enjoy passing on my grandpa's wisdom to the participants through sharing my knowledge via life-changing experiences that working on a farm has brought me."

When working as a farm coach, it is Alyssa's job to build relationships and equip SHALOM farm participants in the context of working with the gardens and animals: alpacas, goats, chickens, ducks, rabbits, and sheep.

The Collisons' son Michael explains the enduring legacy of Glen:

If you lived next door, you would know Glen Collison as the neighbor worth getting to know; quick with a hand, fresh produce, baked goods, or a tractor. If you visited Haven Church you'd find Glen, faithfully serving and leading. He might be anywhere in the building armed with his Bible, props, food, and possibly an accordion. If you attended the Collisons' weekly Sunday school class at Haven, you'd not forget the object lessons of an admitted self-taught teacher.

If you were hurting or in need, you'd discover a man of compassion, who was quick to listen and willing to put skin in the game. And should you have special needs, you encountered an able caregiver who worked diligently to make you feel at home.

If you spent time in Glen's store, you would see how much he loved to market, merchandise, and cut meat. If you walked around his farm, you couldn't miss his passion for plant and animal, soil and fruit, wool, milk, and eggs. If you wandered through his work area, you would be amazed and laugh at the variety of projects undertaken.

Whether working with wool, canning, cooking maple syrup, arranging flowers, making music, or cooking for large groups, you'd be awed at the breadth of his creative interests and efforts. Most of all, if you spent time in Glen's home, you would have no doubt enjoyed his hearty laughter and received some of his generous encouragement.

You would have experienced an unassuming man who lived with a casual grace, unforced spirituality, and personable style that was truly rare and precious. He will be missed by his family, extended family, neighbors, friends, church, and community.

Chapter 14 Challenge: God's name is *Jehovah Tsidkenu*: Lord of truth, justice, equity, doing what is right. Jeremiah 23:6[1]

It was said of Glen, "He paid attention to people, who to the rest of the world, wouldn't matter, and he made them feel that they mattered."

Find someone in your community who needs help and "put some skin in the game."

E.M. Bounds "The word of God is the food by which prayer is nourished and made strong."[2]

---

[1]   Ibid., 8.

[2]   E. M. Bounds, "Prayer Resources," Prayer Coach, May 18, 2011, sponsored by Josiah's Covenant, all rights reserved, https://prayer-coach.com/prayer-resources/

CHAPTER 15

Welcome Home

F ebruary 9, 2018. Sara and I chatted over the phone this Thursday due to another incoming Michigan snowstorm!

She commented quite excitedly, "This week Ferris State University [Big Rapids, MI] is showing our movie about The Ottawa County [Michigan] Community Haven Project.[1] My daughter Julie and I were interviewed for this documentary! There is quite a long story behind it, but this is where we got our training for everything we did at SHALOM."

---

[1] Joshua Pardon, and Marjorie Viveen, *The Poor Farm: A Documentary*, DVD, produced by Joshua Pardon and Marjorie Viveen, (Ottawa County Parks Foundation in association with Ferris State University, Big Rapids, MI, 2017)

She went on to explain that in May of 1978, Glen was hired first for the dairy farm at Ottawa Community Haven (1866 *Poor Farm*). By December of that year, they were hired as acting directors but became permanent directors. By 1987, Glen and Sara would advocate for higher quality care in a group home setting (the first Homestead), having gleaned important lessons from their Community Haven years (1978 to 1987) before SHALOM. The Community Haven (Poor Farm) model, however, was rooted in the early days of Michigan Territory Law (1830) requiring "county boards of supervisors to erect poorhouses to provide relief to poor and distressed families."[2] The job title *Overseer of the Poor* was established by a 1780s northwest territory government. A man had the formal job of determining who was *poor or distressed.*

By 1827, the territorial laws stated, "each [Michigan] township was to care for its own poor, and two Overseers of the Poor were among the town officers. Thus, the smallest division of the territory was made the poor district and keep of the poor left to the lowest bidder. However, by 1830, a poor house or House of Reformation was established per each county, so the task was no longer auctioned off to the lowest bidder."[3]

The poor house was a prodigious improvement. The antiquated label "poor farm or House of Reformation" still sounded very dismal, so it was good to see that Ottawa County changed the 1866 title of poor farm to Community Haven by the 1970s (My father-in-law was orphaned to a "Home for the Friendless.") The Ottawa County *Poor Farm*, however, also had paying boarders, like Judge David Fletcher Hunton. Although once a brilliant, wealthy, famous lawyer, married four times, he eventually was "alone, infirm, with no one to care for him each day." His poems mirror that message: "how swiftly life slips away, like leaves on a river past."[4] Likewise, Michael Collison recounts his father's *swift flight* to eternity but notes that Glen was

---

[2]   Michigan Department of Human Services, DHS Pub-159 (1–11).

[3]   Webster Cook, *Michigan, Its History and Government* (New York, The Macmillan Company, 1905), 204–205.

[4]   "Lonely Old Man, Once a Friend of Daniel Wester, Charles Sumner, Ben Butler, Writes Worthy Verse," 2018, Sandhillcity, http://www.sandhillcity.com/d_f_hunton.htm

neither alone, isolated nor friendless: "In his earlier-than-expected departure, Dad's gifts became even clearer. He welcomed and loved our spouses as much as my brother and sister, offering as much time and attentiveness as any blood relative. Any evaluation of a final rug or blanket or table runner must come after the strings are cut and tied, after the item is off the spindle and on the floor or table or lap. For the first time, I can see Dad's life with depth and clarity. It is off the loom, with no further rows to be pulled, no additional line or color coming. It's done... Here I sit, never questioning my father's love nor his blessing... And while funerals can often demand many an obligatory condolence, there appeared a host of people who loved Dad and [who] had experienced the same from him. Hundreds of people he loved came together."

What makes a man of character like Glen E. Collison? C.S. Lewis proposes, "The Christian does not think God will love us because we are good, but that God will make us good because He loves us."

That love from God was poured out in a life of service to others. Glen worked so hard to keep the dairy farm viable and make it a home! He and the Community Haven residents milked over fifty dairy cows, and their work caring for the 100-head Holstein herd and growing hay to feed cows had made a difference.

Dr. Dee Crittenden writes, "Through their ten years on the Community Haven farm, Glen and his workforce earned several awards for their efforts on the dairy farm. Their milk was richer and in demand. All their milk was carried in buckets by hand. There never was any streamlining of the farm, just many repairs to existing buildings and equipment."[5]

Earning a livelihood on a dairy farm was a critical step forward for so many residents who wanted to be independent. What did previous solutions look like? Well, in 1903, our Michigan Legislature voted on $3,440,616.37 for expenditures for reformatory, penal, pauper, and *eleemosynary* (charity) institutions. The author in 1905 boasted, "We are now able to see that the State of Michigan makes magnificent provision for all classes of its *unfortunate citizens* [indigent poor, ordinary poor, mentally insane, criminally insane, inmates, orphans, old soldiers and their dependents, the blind, deaf, and the dumb, and children of

---

[5] Crittenden, 2007.

sound mind and body]. Scarcely a country in the world can make such a showing!"[6]

Glen and Sara's *eleemosynary* nonprofit SHALOM Inc. organization would improve upon the *magnificent provision* since a "Poor person" was defined as "A person who does not have property, exempt or otherwise, and who is unable because of physical or mental disability or age, to earn a livelihood."[7]

Apparently, Ottawa County Poor Farm had this unique beginning:

Daniel Realy and Great Lakes ship captain Henry Miller bought the land from the federal government. A year later, Realy sowed Ottawa County's first recorded wheat crop at the farm.

In 1842, a Midway House (Inn) was built to accommodate a growing number of travelers (midway) between Grand Rapids and Grand Haven. The property (renamed the Poor Farm) was sold to the (Ottawa) county in 1866. The poor farm's first pauper, John Atwell, was admitted in March that year. The original leather-bound journal kept by the farm's first manager, H.S. Taft, is kept in the Holland Museum archives. It contains notes on each inmate of the farm, including basic information, descriptions on how each person got there and other subjective observations. The (1866) farm, (with the Victorian style brick Ottawa Infirmary building added 1886) was later renamed Community Haven in the 1970s and later operated as a nursing home and was the last of its kind in Michigan when it was shuttered (closed for business) in 2000 as part of the Hope Network.[8]

Since 2000, the Community Haven was renamed as the Eastmanville Farm County Park, a 229-acre county park with horse and

---

6 Cook, 209.

7 Chapter 401, "The Poor Law and Relief and Support of Poor Persons, Act 146 of 1925, effective August 27, 1925," Legislative Council, State of Michigan, 1925, accessed February 2018, courtesy of www.legislature.mi.gov

8 Garret Ellison. "No Person Left Behind at Ottawa County Poor Farm Turned PublicPark," Grand Rapids Press, November 28, 2011, http://www.mlive.com/news/grand-rapids/index.ssf/2011/11/no_person_left_behind_at_ottaw.html

hiking trails in 2004.[9] This modern move confirms the 1990s response to home care saw a trend of moving away from government run facilities like Community Haven. Garret Ellison said, "Before being decommissioned [all buildings but the 1928 barn demolished] and converted into a 229-acre county park, the farmstead was a home for those who had nowhere else to go."[10]

From the Midway Inn to the Eastmanville Farm County Park, the purpose had changed with the national need. Sara and Glen were advocates for homecare. Sara demonstrated conviction in that core value when she said, "Realizing that residents do not go home because this is their home, creates a family atmosphere, but it was our home as well. When you live in the same place where you work, it changes your perspective on how to do that!"

They brought that model to the Homestead and eventually to SHALOM. I came to realize what a real homelife meant to so many adult residents with developmental disabilities when I read the testimonies in Sara's memory album from the Homestead's twentieth anniversary banquet and could see fruit from their original Community Haven vision. Here are their stories in their own words:

April 4, 2007: "Hello, my name is Karen, and I really was on boxes and boxes and boxes of Wheaties cereal as the Special Olympian because Glen and Sara took all of us to our practice and came and got us back. So I got to practice a lot and be a really good athlete. Love them [Glen and Sara]. I have lived at the Homestead since 1987. I was there twenty minutes after Hope who got there when it [the Homestead] first opened up.

---

9 The park is located at 7851 Leonard St. and is open year-round, 7 a.m to 10 p.m. in April through October, 7 a.m. to 8 p.m. in November through April. Outdoor Michigan (Myers Enterprises II, 2011–2017), accessed February 24, 2018, http://outdoormichigan.org/feature/2235

10 Ellison, 2011.

Hope was with them at Ottawa County. They care a whole lot about people who need a little extra help with living this life.

"Glen and Sara always have had a lot of patience, and they teach us over and over until we could do lots of things by ourselves. All our care providers really are family. The SHALOM board loves my cookies too. We have parties and picnics and the best trips. We are all good family!"

2007: "Hello, I am Aaron. I came to SHALOM in 1998. Glen taught me so much about taking care of money. Glen worked and worked to make me learn about how you can only spend what you have. He is a great friend to us all. We love to do tricks on Glen sometimes for fun because he has the best laugh. We are all family here. We like that a lot. We have the best birthdays and holiday times. All our food is really good. Julie cooks for us all the time now, and she cooks just like Glen and Sara. That's because they are Julie's folks, and they taught her how. It is really good eating!

"This is a great house! We like it that we get to see our friends that live with the folks who live in the homes. We see everybody. We go to the YMCA to swim. We are trying to do good things to help everybody because Jesus is so happy when we care about other people. We are all God's children, even the ones we don't know yet. My mother doesn't worry about me because I am safe here and one of the family and she knows that we are taught to look out for each other and everybody else. Glen and Sara are the ones who smile for every person and love everybody around."

2007: "Hello. Meet Mark, Ellen, and Angie. If you want to come meet us, we will have a big picnic and invite all our friends so you can meet everybody. We learn to be responsible people. We like to learn things, to make woven crafts. We do laundry and keep things clean."

"Hello. I am Diane. We hatch baby chicks and baby ducks in the incubator—do you know how *good* we are to take such good care of our baby animals? I love to take their food and water. I have taken on the work of gathering our chicken eggs, candling them, and selling them. I am doing good work to help people feel special. It makes me feel special."

"Hello, I am Sue Smith. The Groveland Home was donated by me [1997] when my mother died and went to heaven. [Sue Smith is in heaven too.] Tom comes every Friday night to get us for our Friday supper and time at the YMCA, and once in a while Dee can come and we go shopping or to a movie or out for ice cream. We live on the bus line that comes to get us to go to work. Don't you think it is so nice that we have so many friends and so much fun? We Groveland ladies sell Taste of Heaven Popcorn and earn our money for trips. This year we are going to Nashville and maybe to see Elvis's House. I know when people give you their money, they really love you a lot. Glen and Sara have a network to help all the homes in our area and even people living at home with relatives. It is so much fun to have so many friends. We have the best trips—we even play games riding on the bus. Laughter really is the best medicine!"

In 2008, Jack Hoogendyk (Michigan House of Representatives in 2003–2008, 61st district) wrote, "Their extended families have benefitted greatly from Sara's close watch [as a registered nurse] of their daily health and well-being. The best of good food prepared from scratch has always been the rule at every meal. Both Glen and Sara are dynamite cooks. Preparing the vegetables for the freezers to enjoy throughout Michigan's long winter is a time of great fun and togetherness. Glen sews too!" (Jack also noted at length the joy of seeing residents gain self-esteem by building independence, weaving on looms, carding wool, and creating projects with wool.)

"Hello from Hope. Dear Glen and Sara, I love you, love you! I remember the homelike atmosphere."

2007: "Hello from DeAnna. Dear Glen and Sara, I have many/many tender thoughtful memories, but you know me, I especially love the silly ones: me trying to corral escaped sheep, you rescuing me from a bat, there are many more, but I will always remember your part in bringing me to SHALOM Homestead and allowing me to achieve my dreams."

I felt so blessed reading all these messages. Sue's comment struck a chord: "I know when people give you their money, they really love you a lot." SHALOM Inc. exists by this miracle of love. The residents know this. Their faith is amazing.

Well, Phil Vlietstra (SHALOM board member) and the team came home joyful from the Guatemala trip just in time to help residents with the sugar maple syrup production. Phil tapped the trees (put in spiles) and the sap was pouring out of them. His wife Judy told me, "It's an odd season again this year, so we have to wait and see what happens."

Residents at SHALOM clearly understand that "maple syrup production is weather dependent [and trust *Jehovah Jireh* for His Provision]. Ideally, sap will flow best on days that are warm [forty-five degrees] and nights that are below freezing. Last year [2017] was an exceptional and record-breaking year for Michigan sap/syrup production when [the state] produced 123,000 million gallons of the sweet stuff! Sunny days are better than cloudy days for increased sap production because the sunlight will hit the trunk of the tree, warming the tree and encouraging the sap [that is stored in the tree's root system during the winter] to be drawn up the trunk toward the top or crown of the tree."[11]

Just as late winter weather was sending maple syrup rushing toward spring, Julie (Kortz) Stevens, Sara's daughter and caregiver at the Homestead, called me with sad news and a request in light of that news. She asked me if I could play the piano (Sunday, February 25) for a memorial service at the Shepherd Barn.

As Judy Vlietstra (SHALOM volunteer and wife of Phil) said, "We lost a dear resident. [Todd Johnson lived at the Homestead.] He was such a gentle man. The resident community weeps with his passing but rejoices in his going home where he will be perfect in every way. I miss him already, but I'm confident he's with Jesus."

I like that loving phrase "resident community." Todd found *shalom* and a home on earth, brothers and sisters in Christ, but now he has an eternal home in the community with the saints. He is meeting Billy Graham this week in heaven! At Todd's memorial, Pastor Keith Lohman spoke to the grieving residents, volunteers, and Todd's family, "Todd is now meeting the Savior saying *Thank you for my life.*" Psalm 139:15–17 tells us that God wrote our life like a book, He saw us before we were born and knows the "number of our chapters." The last chapter is "Homecoming." God alone knows exactly when that last chapter gets

---

11   "Maple Sugaring in Pure Michigan," Michigan Economic Development Corporation 2018, https://www.michigan.org/blog/events/maple-sugaring-in-pure-michigan

written. *"You planned how many days I would live. You wrote down the number of them in your book before I had lived through even one of them."*

As we sang hymns, cried tears, and listened to the memories with some joyful laughter, Pastor Keith had some thoughts for us on *The Inabilities of Disabilities!*

We see what disabilities can do—how disabilities limit and imprison and steal. Now consider what disabilities cannot do: They cannot disable joy or peace, hope or real love. They cannot limit kindness or goodness, generosity or creativity. They cannot stop dreams or determination, imagination or friendship. They cannot prevent gentleness or kindness, curiosity, humor or significance. Disabilities are so limited. Why let them prevail through ignorance and fear, apathy and shame? When we let them—they overwhelm us and make us afraid. When we let them be stronger than patience and acceptance, love and celebration—they overwhelm and make us afraid. Disabilities are so weak. They cannot disable the soul! With God's help, we will not let them disable our souls. Let us celebrate our abilities as we live incredibly free. *Shalom!*

Sara and Glen had also pursued the Ottawa County Community Haven Project (1978–1987) with this very eternal hope in mind—to carry the gospel to an underserved population. They brought this same future vision with them to the Homestead (1987) and eventually to SHALOM Inc. (1990 to present).

I wondered about the original vision of the 1866 Poor Farm. I learned that people were in great need since, "Without Social Security [pre-August 14, 1935], Medicaid or a safety net of any kind for those too poor, too infirm or too old to take care of themselves, the Ottawa County Poor Farm was there."[12]

Joshua Pardon, the Ferris State University professor and documentary moviemaker, worked with three Ferris students to make the movie (DVD) that Sara had given me to watch. "They used footage they shot during last year's [2016] sesquicentennial celebration of the Poor Farm

---

[12] Andrea Goodell, "Celebration Planned for Poor Farm's 150th Anniversary," Holland Sentinel, September 20, 2016, http://www.grandhaventribune.com/History/2016/09/20/Celebration-planned-for-150th-anniversary-of-Ottawa-County-Poor-Farm

along with historical photos and documents to preserve 'the story of the Poor Farm and the life stories of some of its many residents.'"[13]

The movie offers "vignettes on changing the trajectory of a life story from homelessness and hopelessness to inclusion in a community."[14] I could not wait to watch Sara's video to see how some would answer God's question "*What is in your hand?*"

Chapter 15 Challenge: I am *Jehovah Nakeh*—the Lord who smites (from the Hebrew meaning he figuratively disables the proud, making them contrite or lame, no longer able to stand up proudly before Him. Ezekiel 7:9)

It is not a physical disability but a spiritual disability which keeps a person from entering the heavenly home. Matthew Henry affirms, "Sooner or later, sin will cause sorrow, and those who will not repent of their sin, may justly be left to pine away in it. There are many whose wealth is their snare and ruin, and the gaining of the world is the losing of their souls. Riches profit not in the day of wrath. The wealth of this world has not that in it which will answer the desires of the soul or be any satisfaction to it in a day of distress."[15]

What keeps you standing proudly instead of humbly kneeling before the cross?

In Romans 14:11 "It is written: 'As surely as I live,' says the Lord, 'every knee will bow before me, every tongue will acknowledge God.'"

[13] Jeffery Cunningham, "Documentary on Ottawa County Poor Farm to be Shown at Coopersville Library," Sparta, MLive Media Group, June 19, 2017, http://www.mlive.com/sparta/index.ssf/2017/06/documentary_on_ottawa_county_p.html

[14] Joshua Pardon, and Marjorie Viveen, *The Poor Farm: A Documentary*, DVD, produced by Joshua Pardon and Marjorie Viveen, (Ottawa County Parks Foundation in association with Ferris State University, Big Rapids, MI, 2017).

[15] "Bible Hub," Concise Commentary on the Whole Bible by Matthew Henry, accessed online, http://biblehub.com/commentaries/mhc/ezekiel/7.htm

My piano student Katie Stowe, adopted by American Christians at birth, was born without hands but plays piano! When her mom first brought her to me for lessons at a very young age, she hoped that I could teach her to read the treble clef, so she could play her notes for choir. (She was content to just *find notes* on her own as she has an amazingly good ear for pitch.) When she took off her little coat, I realized she had no hands, but this small child looked at me maturely and said, "It is okay, Mrs. Wendt. I do not have hands, but God gave me arms. Would you like a hug? I can do that." That hug melted my heart like a gift from heaven. Humbled by her courage, I took on the task of teaching her. In turn, she humbly practiced all thirty scales (all possible major and minor keys) and eventually drilled scores from Bach to Beethoven! Katie and I now like to joke around and say that had she not humbly learned to read music, she would have been "musically disabled."

Here is her music with a sample of her amazing artwork at the end of the video. https://www.youtube.com/watch?v=ChT_XRKDGxw

While the eyes of the world watched the political turmoil around the athletes in the Winter Olympics in South Korea, I thought about Korean orphans like Katie's adopted brother. Here is a video of Buddy and Katie playing a duet that they arranged to surprise me at lessons! They are my gold medal winners. (Buddy can read all thirty keys too!) https://www.youtube.com/watch?v=4sn8rLPXkFE

What "disables" you from learning in humility?
Focus on what you can do, not on what you cannot do.
What is in your hand? Give it back to God for his glory.

CHAPTER 16

From Another Point of View

Today, I enjoyed brewing "Grog" for Judy Vliestra, my SHALOM friend visiting in *real facetime*. I soon realized that my coffee tasted different from the coffee Sara served. It seems I bought *Grog* coffee with one G, unlike Sara's Grogg with two Gs. What a difference one letter can make: aptitude (I can) or attitude (I won't)!

Like different tastes in coffee, people have different tastes in independence too. Sara Collison wrote in *The Link*, "Independence is different to different people. Too many people associate failure with not having your own apartment. Sometimes your own apartment can be a prison."[1]

The article hosted by The Disability Resource Center adds, "In a group home setting, residents live with people who share accomplishments, activities and goals. Alone in an apartment, a person may feel lonely or secluded. At the Homestead, for example, the residents take on many different hobbies. Some garden, some raise chickens and rabbits, others learn to cook, play instruments, or make maple syrup."[2]

Sara reaffirmed, "We all have some type of job in the community. Residents are quite active because we try to give each person as many independent opportunities as possible. We don't do for people

---

[1] Sara Collison, "Independence Is a Choice: Life in a Foster Care Home," *The Link*, p. 1, The Disability Resource Center, 4026 South Westnedge, Kalamazoo, MI 49008.

[2] Ibid.

what they can do for themselves. It would be a shame to have you not do what you can do."[3]

A job? A career? A vocation? A skill? A talent? A mission?—this article presented so many levels yet one key fact—adults need meaningful *work*. Defining *work*, however, offers as many variations as defining *independence*.

Judy Vlietstra had brought me homemade beeswax lotion bars as a gift for our autistic granddaughter who said, "Oh, Nana, thank Mrs. Vlietstra. I know this lotion with beeswax is really going to *work* because there are no lazy bees. They all *work* and do a job! This lotion is going to work too."

I made Sara laugh when I shared the beeswax story, but she sympathized with creating a work/learning plan which accommodates a literal mind. Our granddaughter was very young when she would ask for a "sheet of white toast and a cup of warm chicken breath" apparently mixing sight, smell, and taste with her words. (Sheet of white paper/sheet of white toast/chicken broth makes smelly breath.) She also made her kindergarten reading teacher laugh when she refused to read the phonics style Nonsense Words—"num, nup, nat, nok, nop, no, no, no." Hands on her hips, she told her teacher, "I am *not* here to learn Klingon."

But no one was laughing when she started writing whole words backwards and reading upside down. We sought out help. Glen understood how difficult these learning challenges can be. Sara relayed how she and Glen had also become an advocate for another young student like this, their daughter Julie! Ruth Van Zyl, the daughter of Julie's Pastor was working on a Master's degree, studying dyslexia. Using a pan of sand to help her see the word, feel the word and hear the word, she successfully taught Julie how to read. The school principal feared she would never read, but she did! Glen and Sara knew she was intelligent and so persisted, in what Sara called, "A pre-diagnosis era." Glen was dyslexic too. I came to admire even more his success in teaching reading.

Well, before Judy and I sat down to watch the *Ottawa County Poor Farm* video, we first loaded up a DVD on Shalom, made in 1995. We heard compassionate testimonies from Shirley and Tom Hill, board member and fundraiser and family members to Steve.

---

[3] Ibid.

We also heard testimonies from founding board member Sally Lindsay, who also had a son with disabilities. "It's not easy, but one on one, we want individuals to see the contributions the residents can have in their lives. One on one, we hope to expand outward to be a community connector."[4]

Erin and Jack Hoogendyk found this to be true when they first volunteered for respite care for Dan and Holly Collison, the caregivers at Homestead North. Then Jack surprised his wife by saying he thought they might be good caregivers too and might want to try that. A host of community workers built the SHALOM Polk Street House where they would soon take on that role.

Sara concurs, "I think they [Erin and Jack] found out that we have a richness in our life that they really wanted to be a part of. They felt their children would also benefit [as the Collison children did] from living with others and learning to interact with residents."[5]

Jack, who served 2003 to 2008 in our Michigan House of Representatives, has been married to Erin since April 4, 1976, has five children and as of June 2012, had eleven grandchildren. He moved to Wausau, Wisconsin in June 2013 to become the executive director of Hope Life Center, www.hopewi.org.

Jack explained their caregiver role at SHALOM, "We still have a level of privacy and a cozy feel since residents have private rooms too. We take the guys with us to high school basketball games, picnics, potlucks, and church functions. For me, it is a great opportunity to have an example for others by the way we interact with them because a lot of people think you have to treat them differently somehow, but they find out that they really don't."[6]

Stanley was their first resident. In the video interview he said, "I love it here. I live at SHALOM because it is *my* home."[7]

Judy, wife of SHALOM board member Phil Vlietstra, mentioned to me while watching the movie together "Oh, yes, I remember Stanley. He would always raise his hands in the air and tell God—*I love you!*"

---

[4] SHALOM Inc, *Making a Difference*, DVD, 1995, Lawrence Productions, with special thanks to Al Dixon, Shalom supporter, Continental Lanes, Dave and Karen Fowler, Rick Connelly, store manager at Pizza Hut, and to Kristen Curnow, store manager at Taco Bell.

[5] Ibid.

[6] Ibid.

[7] Ibid.

Stanley would talk to people about heaven and worship. I remember him thanking me once for playing for a group choir which sang in the community at Christmas. He introduced himself to me with his hand in the air, telling me that he loved to sing hymns and that his mother was in heaven, very proud of him. Stanley made worship seem glorious, as if we were standing next to Jesus.

SHALOM resident Bob also left a good testimony, keeping a work routine faithfully for years at Pizza Hut. His manager mentioned how he was so dependable that he did not require extra supervision like some employees. Erin Hoogendyk also knew the joy of helping residents to find their talents and encouraging them to use them in the community, "You have to find out what the residents are able to do, not sell them short or force them to do something they are unable to do. It takes time to find out what they are good at."[8]

I gained another point of view when I was asked to play for the SHALOM memorial service for Todd. I had quick and efficient tech help from Sara's grandson Noah Kortz, the SHALOM Polk Street house manager and a SHALOM coach. Looking back now, I guess I did not need to come an hour early for *setup*! However, as soon as the keyboard was connected, residents Calvin and Diane just wanted to start singing right away. We got a hymnbook, and they found familiar hymns! They sang so well too. As to having a tech sheet tell us to "sing an hour-long prelude," before the service began, well, I can't say that was part of the formal gig request to come and play. However, experiencing the spontaneous joy of suddenly joining a musical fellowship in praise was such wonderful grief therapy; we were seeking *shalom* together.

After being at several events now, I am amazed by the synergy in the group. The SHALOM Network 2018 has seven homes: Homestead, SHALOM Three Pines, Homestead South, SHALOM Polk, SHALOM Growing Grace, SHALOM Groveland and SHALOM Hope Grove (renamed in 2017, the former home of Roger who lived alone with support from SHALOM), home to forty residents, plus care providers and their families. Three homes are licensed AFC (Adult Foster Care) homes and four are self-determined, supported living homes. The homes are each managed by Christian care providers and operate as extended family, giving residents a place to call home with the support they need.

---

[8] Ibid.

The SHALOM Three Pines home took on new life with the establishment of supported living for men. Men with various developmental disabilities, calling themselves "house brothers," first contracted with Teressa Foster, (and her family—Jerry, Greg, Aaron, and Justin) for basic support in their quest for self-determination and supported independence. (Ryan Smit has been the house manager at SHALOM Three Pines, since 2017.)

The following testimony, from the "house mom's point of view," tells Teressa's story as God unfolded His plan for this home for "brothers!"

1. *What caused you to consider and accept becoming a house mom?* "God opened those doors for me. As the idea was presented to me, and I met the families involved, I became more aware that SHALOM Three Pines was a work of God, bringing people together that need the benefits and brotherhood of *shalom.*"

2. *How have you seen God at work?* "Placing five least likely compatible persons under one roof, and it works! Providing the resources to meet needs. The relationships we have formed."

3. *What is it like being a house mom?* "We are a family, learning from one another. Everyone brings personal knowledge to the house that they can share. Residents had to adjust to a 'different than home—it's not like mom would do it' atmosphere! The support from SHALOM is incredible. I still have my privacy and family life, and I still enjoy the outside activities I did before SHALOM Three Pines. I have had to learn to be more flexible with my personal time."

4. *What do you actually do as a house mom?* "I am responsible for maintaining a safe and Christian home, monitoring of daily chore schedules, planning and preparing nutritious meals, shopping, maintaining a calendar, helping to arrange transportation for activities and work, communicating concerns to SHALOM and parents, monitoring overall health of residents, working with the household budget and balancing bank accounts. I encourage each resident to live to their full potential and show them how."

5. *What are some highlights and joys?* "Every day brings a new joy, every challenge that someone overcomes is so gratifying, especially knowing that I was a part of the team helping the guys grow into independence, witnessing the building of relationships and sharing joys and triumphs."

6. *What are the challenges?* "Learning the habits, likes and dislikes of every resident i.e., food, TV shows, activities, as well as personalities, keeping a regular schedule, helping the parents to accept the changes in their sons' lives, and allow them to grow and overcome challenges independently."

7. *What surprises you the most?* "How difficult it is for us, as parents, to let go, and at the same time how everyone is adjusting. The guys are all happy and want to stay at SHALOM Three Pines. They love it here."

8. *How does it mesh with work?* "It doesn't interfere with work at all."

9. *How does it work for your son, Justin?* "He is thrilled to have 'brothers' to hang out with, and he's learning from them."

10. *Is there a Bible verse that stands out to you in this experience so far?* "Proverbs 3:5–6 'Trust in the Lord with all your heart and lean not on your own understanding, in all your ways acknowledge him, and he will make your paths straight.'"

At the Homestead's thirtieth anniversary party, October 2017, Pastor Keith Lohman asked an intriguing question, "Hey, Julie and Doc, how many van trips were taken to bring residents to multiple events and activities in over thirty years?"

Do the math! Eleven residents, at just a five-trip average per day, yes weekends too, would be 383,250 trips! (Note: all trips taken one at a time.) Wow! How many miles is that? How many loads of laundry? With sixteen family members, at say two loads per week each, that would be 49,920 loads, collecting, washing, drying, folding, putting your stuff away! How many towels is that? How many washers worn out?

Last question: How many meals does thirty years of service represent? At sixteen family members, three meals per day, that would be a whopping 525,600 meals served! Well, here is a question without a number. How much love was poured into people's lives over thirty years? How much patience? How much joy shared? How many prayers lifted? How many lives changed a degree of glory at a time?

Who knows that number? Well, here is that lesson from a different point of view. Who knows everything you do? Hebrew 6:10–12 teaches, "For God is not unjust so as to forget your work and the love which you have shown toward His name, in having ministered and in still ministering to the saints. And we desire that each one of you show the same diligence so as to realize the full assurance of hope until the end, so that you will not be sluggish, but imitators of those who through faith and patience inherit the promises."

Chapter 16 Challenge: God's name is *Elohim.* The first name of God given in the Old Testament: "In the beginning, God [*Elohim*] created the heavens and the earth" (Gen.1:1). The name *Elohim* is unique to Hebraic thinking—it occurs only in Hebrew and in no other ancient Semitic language.[9]

Only God can create. Satan can *only imitate.*

In her winning Right to Life Speech for Michigan, my piano student Katie Stowe offers a precious view of God's creation, "I was safe. Safe from chemicals, instruments, abortions, murderous crime. No one knew who I would be, or what I would look like. No ultrasounds. No tests. No judgments. I was safe in my mother's womb. No one saw that my legs were not fully forming. No one saw that there were not ten little fingers. In fact, no one even saw that there were no hands. I was safe. Dr. Ben Carson has spoken out about how unsafe a mother's womb has become. He said, 'Millions upon millions of innocent little human beings who have no chance of defending themselves are placed in the safest environment that God could place them in. And we have found a way to go in there and murder them.'"[10]

Psalm 139 confirms, "Oh yes, you shaped me first inside, then out, you formed me in my mother's womb. I thank you, High God—you're breathtaking! Body and soul, I am marvelously made! I worship in adoration—what a creation! You know me inside and out, you know every bone in my body. You know exactly how I was made, bit by bit, how I was sculpted from nothing into something. Like an open book, you watched me grow from conception to birth, all the stages of my life were spread out before you, the days of my life all prepared before I'd even lived one day."[11]

---

[9]   "Elohim," Theopedia, accessed March 2018, https://www.theopedia.com/elohim

[10]   "Katie Stowe—Speech for Right to Life of Michigan Banquet 2016," YouTube, https://www.youtube.com/watch?time_continue=2&v=EouxwIrMdmU

[11]   Psalm 139:13–17, The Message.

Take time today to understand life from another person's point of view, even from the viewpoint of a baby in the womb. What does it mean to be free, independent, defended, valued, precious to *Elohim*? What is in your hand to accomplish that goal? A job? A career? A vocation? A skill? A talent? A mission?

Additional author's note: Logan Collison, son of Michael and Linda, grandson of Sara and Glen Collison has just been deployed to Afghanistan. The news is just breaking to the public today, as we are submitting the final edit of this book. We asked Logan what he would like our readers to know about his choice to defend life. He shared with honesty that while his initial goal was to enter the army National Guard to pay for college, a new mission has recently reshaped his life. Logan clarifies, "I am upheld to a higher standard when people see me in uniform. Defending the country makes you a better man. When I look around and think of my grandma and friends who cannot take on this choice, I realize that I can do this—I can fight for others to have security and life. I freely choose this. This pathway is my calling! I embrace this with pride and joy." As his military career advances, he also hopes to finish college and be a high school history teacher. Sounding like a true son of his grandfather Glen, Logan concluded, "There are no boring history classes!"

Sara and his family are so proud of Logan and invite you to support and pray for all our military men and women. Thank you to all who defend life from whatever point of view and background God has called you.

CHAPTER 17

In This Time of Our Deep Need

March 1, 2018 at 6191 North Riverview Drive. Well, this past week we sure weathered some odd March weather: the saying goes *in like a lamb, out like a lion*, but what about *in like a flood, out like a fish?* The Kalamazoo River flooded its banks this week on South Riverview Drive; fish were stranded in the street![1]

As I drove up to the SHALOM farm today, some more serious clean-up was also going on in the ashes at the sheep fold. The sheep barn had burned to the ground on that stormy-windy February 25th morning, same day as the funeral memorial day for Todd. Two baby goats had died, but Pastor Keith was thankful that all the sheep ran out safely. However, they were huddled in fear at the far corner of the pen, waiting at the gate for the shepherd to come! They were intuitively drawn to the gate, the farthest point away from flames and danger. Rescuers called it "one big mass of wool" crouched tightly in a massive heap of panic waiting for the shepherd. What a beautiful metaphor to preach on for a funeral. John 10:7–13, "I am the Gate for the sheep. All those others are up to no good—sheep stealers, every one of them. But the sheep didn't listen to them. I am the Gate. Anyone who goes through me will be cared for—will freely go in and out and find pasture. A thief is only

---

[1] Lori Higgins, "Jet Skis Take to the Flooded Streets of Kalamazoo," Detroit Free Press, February 25, 2018, https://www.freep.com/story/news/local/michigan/2018/02/25/video-jet-skis-flood-streets-kalamazoo/371743002/

there to steal and kill and destroy. I came so they can have real and eternal life, more and better life than they ever dreamed of. (The Message)"

I had asked Sara how she felt that day. She said, "Glen had built that barn. Seeing the loss was like losing another piece of him. But you know, when he had a heart attack in 1995, he had to let go of the farm animals, and we had empty stalls then too. He just recited to me Habakkuk 3:17. Julie and I recited the same verse as we embraced."

"Even though the fig trees are all destroyed, and there is neither blossom left nor fruit; though the olive crops all fail, and the fields lie barren; even if the flocks die in the fields and the cattle barns are empty, yet I will rejoice in the Lord; I will be happy in the God of my salvation. The Lord God is my strength; he will give me the speed of a deer and *bring me safely over the mountains.*"

Sara firmly knew that Glen had this confidence because he had seen what God had done already in their life. Habakkuk 3:2: "I worship you in awe for the fearful things you are going to do. In this time of our deep need, begin again to help us, as you did in years gone by. Show us your power to save us."

Sara also told me that she had been praying over the nation this week, "Leah, just look at this timing for Billy Graham's death. I kept asking God, *Why did he suffer so long to live to age ninety-nine, trapped in a failing body with failing health?* It seems he was kept for this very moment [February 21, 2018]. Even in his death, he has a national platform to speak about our need of salvation. His memorial service will offer one final crusade, where even in death, the gospel reaches a global audience."[2]

Sadly, a Valentine's Day school shooting in Florida left gaping wounds of deep need and initiated a unified demand to find solutions, including Mental Health Reform. Citizens gathered at the White House on the very day that Billy Graham had died. As to taking center stage in Washington, Mitch McConnell said it well, "Billy Graham lifted up

---

2   Billy Graham Evangelistic Association (BGEA), "Billy Graham's Final Crusade," BGEA, 2018, https://billygraham.org/story/billy-grahams-final-crusade/

our nation, not because he occupied the spotlight so masterfully—but because he knew he wasn't the one who belonged in it."[3]

I learned from Sara's DVD that the original Ottawa County Poor House (Michigan, 1866) was also established in response to a national outcry to find urgent solutions to a crisis. Wounded Civil War soldiers were coming home after the battles. African American soldiers who had fought in the Union Army like the Ben Jones, were refugees who needed a place "to stay in dignity and not feel abandoned, where they could live in honor for their heroism."[4]

This chapter of anger and upheaval in American history also shines as a light to this generation. Dr. Fred Johnson, Professor of History at Hope College, addressed the core issue by saying Michigan was "helping the invisible who need a caring community who can respond when we are at our best."[5]

The Poor Farm was a tribute to Ottawa County since it was the oldest operating Poor Farm in the United States of America, operating for 130 years! Julie (Kortz) Stevens encouraged those viewing the DVD. "It is important as a society that we slow down to see what we can be a part of—to care for the person next to us, to see what we can be a part of versus life is just *all about us!*"[6]

Slow down—find solutions in community. I see this theme resonating through SHALOM every step of the way. The model Glen and Sara saw at Community Haven was a "working" farm where residents could find meaningful work or benevolence by working the farm. From the old and sick, to the crippled war heroes and local maritime legends, lonely aging residents were offered a social community, proving that they were not abandoned to isolated suffering.

Sara comforted me too when she said, "God is always busy weaving lives together." Themes of "isolation" are all over the news. Solutions always focus on "unity in community." Sara would explain that we are "felted together" to share our strengths. I could see that natural idea in

---

[3] Art Moore, "A Grateful Nations Mourns: Billy Graham Honored at US Capitol," February 28, 2018, WND, http://www.wnd.com/2018/02/a-grateful-nation-mourns-billy-graham-honored-at-u-s-capitol/

[4] Pardon and Viveen, DVD, 2017.

[5] Ibid.

[6] Ibid.

the alpaca dryer balls which I bought in honor of Todd the resident who made them and just passed away. Gently tumbled in the laundry, dryer balls soften the clothing and cut drying time. They can *only do that felted together!* Separately, these fibers are thin and weak, lost strands without purpose. Second Chronicles 7:14 is a call for God's people to *humble and tumble ourselves together,* and seek God's face as a group.

I could see how God had woven Ellen Verberkmos into Glen and Sara's lives. Ellen said, "Glen and Sara wanted residents to have the opportunity to have life skills, work skills, and not just housing [at Community Haven]."[7]

Ellen Verberkmos was Relief Supervisor (1984–1987) and trained the horses with the residents, a perfect match. It reminds me of a Ronald Reagan quote that I heard he liked to use, "There is nothing better for the inside of a man than the outside of a horse!"

Ellen would later be a strong prayer warrior for them in 1987, when Collisons had to leave the farm due to the county's financial instability and shifting priorities.

Giving adults with developmental disabilities a home, meaningful work, an opportunity for inclusion in a community—that was the Collisons' vision for healing the lonely and isolated. All of those lessons were gleaned and carried to SHALOM.

When the Collisons first came to Community Haven in 1978, Sara told me that the board feared the farm might close within a year. Would it become a petting zoo? Just land plots parceled out to developers? Or remain as a 229-acre farm?

Sara detailed their work in the documentary, "Here everyone felt like they belonged. They were needed. This is not just the kind of project you just stop doing. It needs a strong presence in the community."[8]

---

7   Ibid.
8   Ibid.

They took on that challenge. Julie (Kortz) Stevens, daughter of Glen and Sara recalls, "My parents were extremely creative and seemed to make things happen."[9]

She was right. When people hear the word farm, they might think of the hard work and the smell, but the residents enjoyed movie nights, trips to McDonalds, chalk talks, local band concerts, and school events. They would hold bazaars, and residents would attend the school sponsored adult education classes. The community got involved with residents making Christmas so special. Residents soon got to go to a camp with the help of the Community Haven's staff and community education school teachers.

Hope, Mary Lou, Bob, and Sara soon got some puppies and trained leaders dogs for the blind. A church nearby Community Haven, however, had another form of blindness. They asked Glen and Sara not to bring their residents back there to worship.

As Dee Crittenden relays, "The world expanded a little more as they sought and found a church to welcome them to worship. Glen and Sara and their three children [Mike, Dan, and Julie] saw close up and personal the change it makes to have dignity restored, to gain well-deserved self-respect, to be loved and nurtured, and to have joy in life!"[10]

I see that same value endorsed at the new Eastmanville Park (former Community Haven) which has been relabeled "A place of remembrance." The original 1928 Poor Farm barn still in use for historic exhibits, dramatic reenactments, live music, and food. Why should we remember the past?

Here is an unusual story to underscore that point. Dr. Dee Crittenden's husband, Harold, worked in the Collison's Grocery store for Glen's dad Lyle! (Married in 1958, Dee would later be busy with twins by 1961!) Meanwhile, Harold was working in the store and attending college to be a teacher. However, Dee would not meet Glen and Sara until the year 2000, when they would be working together on a farm project in the area. Imagine a pattern woven with two shuttles, two wefts and different color timeline threads in the warp, getting trea-

---

9   Ibid.

10   Dr. Dee Crittenden, "A Celebration of Service in God's Love," SHALOM Inc., 17th Anniversary, 2007. Used with permission by SHALOM Inc., 2018

dled—not a plain weave. Some looms can boast a thousand heddles to pass the warp!

At the Community Haven Sesquicentennial Celebration, 2016, artist Jane Ewing created panels to preserve these woven life memories. The panels hang in the barn and celebrate the lives of the caregivers. I felt a part of history when I saw the Collisons' name engraved on the art panel on display. Also underground radar was used to locate and restore unmarked graves.[11] *Dignity was restored.* Reenactors now retell these life stories to teach the next generation how to value people once lonely and forgotten!

As I watched the documentary video, I suddenly saw the core values in Glen and Sara's mission statement for SHALOM Inc. They believed that God created the unit of *the family* for nurture, safety, and our path to fullest potential. This point was anchored again with the enigmatic story of a resident named Monroe Rutty, renamed by his Ottawa County caregivers as Joe Steel.

On Feb. 25, 1907, a man, half clothed, penniless, and close to hypothermia, was discovered wandering in subzero weather near Lamont. He didn't know who he was, what he was doing or where he was going. His rescuers dropped him off at the Ottawa County Infirmary (Victorian brick building added in 1886 to the Poor Farm), where he was welcomed and named Joe.

Diagnosed as feeble-minded but classified *insane,* "Joe" was a harmless, sweet man whom staff and other residents came to love. He worked plowing the farm on the infirmary property and enjoyed tinkering with related machinery."[12]

May 13, 1965, Joe's nephew saw the photo of the man without an identity [with amnesia] published in the Holland Sentinel and recog-

11 Ron Cammel, "Forgotten Cemetery for Ottawa County Poor Farm Gets New Recognition with Park Improvements," Grand Rapids Press, October 2, 2009, http://www.mlive.com/news/grand-rapids/index.ssf/2009/10/forgotten_cemetery_for_ottawa.html

12 Kevin Collier, "111-year-old Resident Was Man Without An Identity," Grand Haven Tribune, July 21, 2015, http://www.grandhaventribune.com/News/2014/03/31/111-year-old-resident-was-039-man-without-an-identity-039

nized him and said he was their lost Uncle Monroe Rutty! Rutty lived happily to be 111 (1860-1971).

Why is this thread so important to the SHALOM Inc. tapestry?

Sara told me that Glen loved to read about these Poor Farm stories. He loved history and that was evident by his family scrapbook dating generations back to the 1800s. President Nixon sent a letter of congratulations to Monroe Rutty on his life of longevity at the farm.[13] In an era before POTUS twitter, presidential letters were saved and valued. In 1972, my blind Syrian immigrant grandmother wanted me to write a letter to President Nixon for her (we got a response). She loved American freedom and the ability for her children (born in America) to run a boardinghouse. Anna Teisan (the English name randomly assigned to her at Ellis Island) lived to be ninety-eight! Jesus's face was the first face she saw, since she prayed to follow Christ while listening across the hall when a pastor came to her boarding house to pray over a dying boarder. She died 2001.

So why does Monroe Rutty's lifestory of longevity like my grandmother's story also strike me as so profound? This story supports Glen and Sara's premise that quality care in an extended family style setting can bring greater happiness, meaningful labor, a means of independence, and inclusion in a community which offers stability.

Glen and Sara added spiritual depth and explained, "Adults with developmental disabilities also need to broaden a circle of friends, activities, and trips to provide a much higher quality of home care. Further gratification comes when you see them grow and change and develop maturity."[14]

These values formed the current SHALOM Inc. Mission statement: We are Christian people working with caring communities to provide housing, social and educational opportunities for adults with developmental, physical, emotional, and mental disabilities. To accomplish that mission, SHALOM Inc. will do the following:

- Maintain a family living environment that will encourage a vital and productive lifestyle for adults with disabilities, encouraging work and/or educational opportunities.

---

[13] Pardon and Viveen, DVD, 2017.
[14] Ibid.

- Recognize the importance and value of the whole person and create a nurturing environment for adults with disabilities through the love of Christ.
- Integrate community, free enterprise, unique talents and extended family, thereby cultivating sufficient resources to fulfill its mission and enable adults with disabilities to experience SHALOM—peace within.
- Provide opportunities of recreation, travel, and experience for adults with disabilities in our community with volunteers, community leaders, and caregivers.

For the Collisons, those values were shaped in the furnace of trials at Community Haven. According to the 2017 documentary, the Social Security Act of 1935 would bring new changes to the *Poor Farm*, which had previously been the only safety net for aging citizens with no means for care. Community Haven's purpose would later transition again with the Michigan's Adult Foster Care Facility Licensing Act of 1979, embracing the trend toward group homes.

Before I left the farm today, Sara walked quickly into the "Glory Room" and called for me to come see what was happening outside. I was retrieving my wet tennis shoes from the heat vent where Sara had lovingly placed them after my rain-puddle-jumping-entry this morning. Gigantic snowflakes like fluffy cotton balls were dropping from the sky! Sara and I felt like we were trapped inside a snow globe! We both agreed that we had never seen snowflake "balls" quite like this before. Did the Israelites feel like this in the desert of Egypt? A food called *manna* fell from the sky; *manna* literally means "What is it?" They were hungry but did not know that God could rain-down perfect food! They had to taste it by faith having never tasted anything like it before. As it says in 1 Corinthians 2:9, "Eye has not seen, nor ear heard, nor have entered into the heart of man, the things God has prepared for those who love him."

Even while Glen was keeping up a heavy workload milking cows, trying to keep the farm financially sound, God knew His provision of the Homestead was on the horizon! In the hour of their deepest need, He was about to provide, like *manna* from heaven raining down on Collisons, despite Ottawa County's shift in priorities. I can't wait to hear how Sara's dad comes back into the timing of this provision. I will ask next Thursday!

In my library collection, I have an original copy of *The Memorial Address on the Life and Character of Abraham Lincoln*, written in 1866, the same year that the Poor Farm was established. George Bancroft wrote, "That God rules in the affairs of men is as certain as any fact of physical science."[15]

That assertion is reflected in the Poor Farm notebook recording names of residents, dates, and a column for notes and/or the cause of "pauperism." A Dutch shoemaker with seventeen children immigrated to Holland, Michigan, with his brother but lost his shoe shop in the great Holland fire of 1871. Becoming an alcoholic, they said he had to leave the church. His great-great grandson, Pastor Gerrit, remarked that "in those days they had no understanding of what it meant to be an alcoholic."[16] Later indigent, he was taken into the Ottawa County Poor Farm 1873, where he became bedridden, but the Poor Farm journal notes that he *died happy* in 1876. The documentary states clearly that he read his Bible daily and died at peace with God in the end years of his life.[17] Pastor Gerrit was grateful to the Poor Farm that his loved one did not die alone drunk in an alley. Instead he found *shalom!*

Chapter 17 Challenge: Jehovah El Gomolah, I am the God of Recompense.[18]

How would our world's timeline change if we obeyed the challenge in God's Word?

---

[15] George Bancroft, "Memorial Address on the Life and Character of Abraham Lincoln," 1866, https://ia800202.us.archive.org/9/items/memorialaddresso01banc/memorialaddresso01banc_bw.pdf

[16] Pardon and Viveen, DVD, 2017, with thanks to research from Fred Johnson, Sara Collison, Julie Stevens, Kurt and Beverly Schroeder, Glen Okonosi, Chris Loughrin, Ellen Denny, Meredith Slover, Gerrit Sheers, Jim Budzynski, Wallace and Jane Ewing, Debra Sturtevant, Robert and Janice Mahaney, Linda Vivian, Katie Van Huis, Geoffrey Reynolds, and Craig Powers.

[17] Ibid.

[18] Simcox, 18

Romans 12. Bless those who persecute you, bless and do not curse. Rejoice with those who rejoice, mourn with those who mourn. Live in harmony with one another. Do not be proud but be willing to associate with people of low position. Do not be conceited. Do not repay anyone evil for evil. Be careful to do what is right in the eyes of everyone. If it is possible, as far as it depends on you, live at peace with everyone. Do not take revenge, my dear friends, but leave room for God's wrath, for it is written: "It is mine to avenge. I will repay," says the Lord. On the contrary: "If your enemy is hungry, feed him. If he is thirsty, give him something to drink. In doing this, you will heap burning coals [like sending comfort, a warm kitchen fire which was a blessing in the days before matches] on his head [reaping a kindness undeserved when pay back was expected]." Do not be overcome by evil but overcome evil with good.

Leah Wendt's mother, Martha Waterlander Teisan, was a little girl when she was hit by a car while working on the celery farm in Decatur. Severely injured with a broken leg, she was rescued by a neighbor who drove her to the doctor. She later became a registered nurse, graduating from West Suburban Nursing School in Wheaton, Illinois. In later years, who should become her elderly patient but the very man who rescued her! Every day she got to repay him, and the Lord was her recompense for every good deed done without applause and fanfare.

How might someone's lifestory or timeline change if you believed in *Jehovah El Gomolah*? How would you treat them or draw them into community?

CHAPTER 18

Prayer: Not My Will but Thine Be Done

When Judy Vliestra and I sat and watched the 1995 SHALOM/ DVD presentation together, we felt so moved watching old footage of Glen standing on the lawn in 1995 just speaking from his heart, "We all have a need to be connected to somebody."[1]

SHALOM Inc. has truly continued this vision of weaving together people for God's glory!

Pastor Lohman recently wrote, "Every week is a new adventure at SHALOM! This past Wednesday, Marcy and Kelly took a group of SHALOM Woolery participants to Great Northern Weaving to pick out new warp string colors for our looms. We bought 120 spools of warp string! It was a great learning experience for everyone. Thanks to the helpful staff for showing us around and giving us a fun, informative tour!"

Glen loved weaving wool mats and rag rugs, sheering, carding and spinning wool and knew how residents would naturally interlock and bond when they worked together on such farm projects, "Further gratification comes when you see each of the individuals change! You

---

[1] SHALOM Inc, *Making a Difference*, DVD, 1995, Lawrence Productions, with special thanks to Al Dixon/Shalom supporter, Continental Lanes, Dave and Karen Fowler, Rick Connelly, store manager at Pizza Hut, and to Kristen Curnow, store manager at Taco Bell.

see them grow, build maturity, enjoy life! That's where the gratification comes."[2]

Sara concurred, "The thing that probably charges us up the most is to see a person change, to become more of what God intended them to be. We are not a program—we're a home offering quality care with extended family commitment. We believe with all our heart this is the way to go."[3]

A quick glance at the current SHALOM website gives you an overview of all the opportunities for volunteers and workers in the SHALOM network. I see the fruit of Glen and Sara's prayers! https://www.shalomkazoo.org/overview

Glen also reflected, "SHALOM would not exist without the parents because they are the ones who can see the vision, the need for their son or daughter to have a place where they can continue to grow, to have people come alongside them, when the day comes that families cannot care for them."

Planning for the future becomes a reality with challenging questions when aging parents like Shirley and Tom Hill, board member and fundraiser, said they had to look to the future. SHALOM became a great answer to prayer for their son Steve. Don and Dorothy Bonnema are also featured in the DVD and mention the blessing of finding a home for her brother Roger Neibor, whom retired State Senator Jack Welborn called "a good neighbor."[4]

Sara observed, "Most people feel that adults with developmental disabilities should stay in their families as that is their responsibility. What we see is that they need emancipation just like anybody else, broadening their circle of friends to do things with, yet they still need their families very much in their lives. We have been blessed to have very strong family support encouraging us in so many ways, being a part of transport [chaperones of field trips] but working alongside of us, so we can provide a greater quality of care for our residents."[5]

So this week, while watching the DVD, we are seeing a younger version of our friend Sara from 1995, but still hearing the same 2018

---

[2] Ibid.
[3] Ibid.
[4] Ibid.
[5] Ibid.

voice. Other than the time warp of twenty years, I still hear my friend being faithful to her first love. She states in the video:

"SHALOM is a ministry about creating opportunities; we want to see lives becoming more independent, more productive, more able to care for themselves. SHALOM was birthed out of the desire to know that there would be continuity of care. We realize the importance of individuals reaching their maximum potential, and they can only do that through the support of others. The name for SHALOM Inc. was chosen through a prayer, asking God to give us the qualities that we want."

Then in March of 1987, Glen suddenly lost his job with Ottawa County Community Haven. That same Friday, Sara was scheduled to go to Kalamazoo to visit her mother, Dorotha Goldstein. It was the first Torah weekend at the synagogue, funded as a memorial to Sara's father, Isadore Goldstein. Shocked and overwhelmed by this added loss, Glen's schedule was now free to be able to go with Sara to the special weekend.

Sara wondered, *In God's foreknowledge, what is He up to? How will God now answer Glen's earnest prayer for direction? Community Haven has been a call on our life and on our family's life. It has also been our home for nine years! We love serving there and do not want to leave.*

Sara further told me "By now we had experienced God's trustworthiness, love, and mercy, and had chosen to walk in faith and obedience. Our call and passion had not really changed, just the circumstances. What next? Foster care? If so, where, when, how?"

Sara's father had been in real estate and had purchased a farmhouse and 190 acres in 1934, turning the mid-nineteenth century pioneer farmhouse into four apartments. Her parents, grandparents, and other family members had lived there until June of 1944, before Sara's birth. By the time of her father's death in December of 1986, the house had fallen into disrepair and was condemned.

During their weekend visit (first Torah weekend), Sara's mom mentioned that the estate properties just became available, and there was already an offer on the Riverview Drive farmhouse, north of Parchment. A contractor wanted to rehab the apartments!

Sara wondered, *Are we to return back to our family roots in Kalamazoo?*

When they went back to Community Haven a couple of days after Torah weekend, they had a sense that God was already at work with a whole new beginning, and they were encouraged. Mike and Dan were at college, and Julie was finishing her sophomore year of high school. Meanwhile, Sara continued to work until June 1, 1987 at Community Haven's Congregate Facility as administrator for the sixty residents.

Praying and searching, God's perfect plan began to unfold just in time with provisions they could never have imagined! God indeed had given Sara's mom a dream with peace (*shalom*) that they were to return to Kalamazoo and resurrect this condemned farmhouse on Riverview Drive. An inheritance gift went into securing the condemned house, with thirteen acres deeded to SHALOM Inc. with the balance of acreage in trust until her mother's death. (She died in 2002.)

For Sara, the miracle of first letting go of the dream at Community Haven brought about the next answer to prayer—the Homestead—right into their open hands, waiting in prayer for direction from the

Lord. They knew God was firmly leading them, *Now what is in your hand? Use it for me.*

The nonprofit's organizational name SHALOM was "chosen through a prayer."[6] How did Sara learn so much about prayer as a young believer? Sara said she had not thought of this lady in years but suddenly remembered her name: Beverly White. Who was she? When Sara was in nurse's training at Bronson School of Nursing in her freshman year, the Bethel Baptist Church's College Group would go together to visit residents in a nursing home in downtown Kalamazoo. One patient there stood out, being bedridden all her life, yet always filled with joy and smiling. Sara admitted that she would walk to the nursing home on her day off, just to spend time with Beverly, even when her friends did not go with her. Beverly showed me the depth of prayer. "My sole purpose is to pray," she confessed to Sara. "I *can* do that."

Sara recalled how, "This joy of hers drew me back to her, again and again. She taught me that we can never claim a disability from serving God!"

The great English preacher, Charles H. Spurgeon (1834–1892) agreed, "As well could you expect a plant to grow without air and water as to expect your heart to grow without prayer and faith. I would rather teach one man to pray than ten men to preach. Prayer girds human weakness with divine strength, turns human folly into heavenly wisdom, and gives to troubled mortals the peace of God. We know not what prayer can do."[7]

This week, instead of meeting on Thursday at our usual time, Sara would be at the hospital having more procedures/tests. She prayed over everything, just like Corrie ten Boom who rescued Jews in the Holocaust (April 15, 1892–April 15, 1983): "Any burden too small to be turned into a prayer is too small to be made into a burden! *Never be afraid to trust an unknown future to a known God.*"[8]

After the tests, Sara sent an email: Leah, It was very challenging! Without the Lord, I would never have made it! I do want to get together next Thursday if at all possible. Continued prayers appreciated! Sara

---

6   Ibid.

7   Charles H. Spurgeon, "Prayer Resources," Prayer Coach, sponsored by Josiah's Covenant, all rights reserved, May 18, 2011, https://prayer-coach.com/prayer-resources/

8   Corrie ten Boom, Ibid.

Months ago, we wanted to write about the topic of prayer, and now suddenly in mid-March 2018, it seemed that God was writing this chapter for us, allowing us to live and breathe the topic of prayer. Today as I type up notes from our last coffee chat by the fire, I see how Sara has always modeled the *prayer warrior mode.* She told me that she loves the simple trust of her residents at SHALOM, "Leah, they do not put up the arguments and obstacles like we often do with God. They just have that pure trust that scripture says we must have."

Luke 18:17 concludes, "Truly I tell you, anyone who will not receive the kingdom of God like a little child will never enter it" (New International Version).

This reminded me of a story. I got invited over for lunch to a friend's house years ago. The long wooden dinner table holds enough chairs to host her family of ten kids plus more guests. I sat down in the chair closest to my friend, but her dismayed-looking children suddenly erupted into whispering! Finally, one of them spoke up softly to warn me that I was sitting in *the naughty chair* closest to their mom! In fact, the good mom just pulled her little ones closer to her whenever they needed more guidance to hear and obey within the noisy family structure. *This* is prayer! Jesus lovingly pulls us closer and quietly whispers exactly what we need to hear over a noisy world.

Corrie ten Boom confirms the blessing of drawing closer, "You may never know that *Jesus* is all you need, until *Jesus* is all you have."

And another email came to draw the ministry supporters to our knees.

Dear Prayer Warriors: I have recently been having a heart issue called atrial flutter. I am now scheduled for an April 10 ablation which should cure it and get me running again at 100 percent. Yes, running. So I am asking for prayer for that outpatient procedure and for the preparation and recovery with blood thinners. I have a Great Physician overseeing the entire process and give Him all the glory. Please also pray as I preach this Palm Sunday [on Isaiah 53] with great calm to keep the flutter in control! Thank you for praying! Pastor Keith, Director, SHALOM Inc.

Sara's week was also filled with more prayer requests. I sent her a note.

Dear Sara, I found this poem on the correct posture for prayer and thought of you since you said you were praying in some awkward positions with MRIs this week. *Shalom* my friend. Praying for you, Leah.

The Prayer Of Cyrus Brown
by Sam Walter Foss (1858–1911)

The proper way for a man to pray, said deacon Lemuel Keyes, "And the only proper attitude is down upon his knees."

"No, I should say the way to pray," Said Rev. Dr Wise, "Is standing straight with outstretched arms and rapt and upturned eyes."

"Oh, no, no no," said Elder Slow, "Such posture is too proud: A man should pray with eyes fast closed and head contritely bowed."

"It seems to me his hands should be, austerely clasped in front. With both thumbs pointing toward the ground," Said Rev. Doctor Blunt.

"Las' year I fell in Hodgkin's well, head first," said Cyrus Brown, "With both my heels a- stickin up, my head a -pointing down;

An' I made a prayer right then an' there--best prayer I ever said, The prayingest prayer I ever prayed, a-standin' on my head."

RE: Leah, Lol! I loved your poem! Sara.

Well, the phone rang the following Thursday morning, but it was Sara's daughter Julie instead, still at the hospital. "Leah, I see a note in my mom's phone here: Meet Leah for book writing, 9:30 a.m. Thurs. You were not expecting her today were you?"

Sara would later tell me that right when Julie and I prayed for her together over the phone at 9:30 a.m., an important resolution came to fix a problem that was critical to complete the test that day. She was suddenly surrounded by several Christian medical professionals who were assisting with solutions/decisions and discovered the resolution for the procedure to continue. And how would they have known that we had prayed for her to be encircled, surrounded by God.

Psalm 125:1–5 boldly tells us, "Those who trust in the LORD *are* like Mount Zion, *which* cannot be moved, *but* abides forever. As the mountains surround Jerusalem, So the LORD surrounds His people from this time forth and forever."

Sara later told me about the discomfort of having procedures done in all sorts of odd positions that make it difficult to breathe. Sara said she was on holy ground thinking of the Savior—arms outstretched suffocating on the cross for our sins. Then came this intense email sent to the church prayer chain. Time stood still as I read it.

On 3/20/2018 8:47 AM, Sara Collison wrote: My dear prayer warriors! Results of biopsy. Cancer. Please pray for God's intervention for His scheduled time and keep me in His perfect peace! *Shalom.* "I waited patiently for the Lord, He turned to me and heard my cry. He lifted me from the pit, He set my feet on a rock and gave me a firm place to stand. He put a new song in my mouth, a hymn of praise to our God. Many will see and fear and put their trust in the LORD!" Psalm 40:1–3.

Dear readers: Sara and I want you to know that we have prayed for you since the first day we started writing this book, September 14, 2017. Our heart's desire was and still is to write His story for His glory.

And now, just as Andrew Murray said, we will pray, "May God open our eyes to see what the holy ministry of intercession is, to which, as His royal priesthood, we have been set apart. May He give us a large and strong heart to believe what mighty influence our prayers can exert. And may all fear as to our being able to fulfill our vocation vanish as we see Jesus, living ever to pray, living in us to pray, and standing surety (as a guarantee or sponsor) for our prayer life."

Do we really believe what a mighty influence our prayers can exert? On May 19, 1997, my husband Roy and I spent our thirteenth wedding anniversary at my father's funeral, in the same church (Decatur Bible Church/Michigan), with the same friends, at the same time that we were married thirteen years earlier—2 p.m. Who but God can orchestrate time like that? Instead of my father giving me away as a bride, I was giving away my sweet Syrian daddy (Robert F. Teisan 1928–1997) offering him back to God to be the *redeemed bride of Christ*, to enjoy Jesus's presence forever. Daddy is now a joint-heir with Christ, walking streets of gold without an amputated leg in a celestial new body. When I helped Mom to set out his clothes for the funeral, I found his favorite spiral notebook in his suitcoat pocket. I cried. My name was written in it, along with prayer notes and grocery lists. And Jesus sent me comfort in answer to his prayer. Romans 8:34, "Christ Jesus who died—more than that, who was raised to life—is at the right hand of God and is also interceding for us."

I love these stories about Christ our High Priest. Sara and I had both read the *Friends of Israel Magazine.* We both had heard about Zvi

Kalisher, who was dropped off at a Polish orphanage by his parents in an effort to save his life. His parents lost their lives in a WWII concentration camp. Zvi, however, hid from Nazis as he crawled back through drains to bring food to Jews trapped in Warsaw. He fought for Israel's independence in 1948 by diffusing bombs. He was called brave. However, when he met *Yeshua*, the Hebrew name for Jesus, he was called *bold as a lion*, witnessing in every corner of Jerusalem, from synagogues to the yeshivas, anywhere.[9]

Zvi Kalisher (1928–2014) writes, "I told them *Mashiach Tzidkenu* [Messiah our Righteousness] is *Yeshua*, our salvation! Only in the Hebrew language does this phrase work in this manner and is considered Kosher."

Zvi continued to share his faith in Messiah with Jews saying, "Yet it bothered them that all I had was one little book [a Bible in Hebrew, even though he spoke nine languages]. They asked me what book I prayed from. I told them that my prayer book is my heart. I come before the Lord and open my heart before Him. And I use no books. I believe the Lord, only according to what is written in the Bible. This is the most important book ever written."[10]

Thursday, March 22, 2018. As I drove up to Sara's cabin at the farm today, myriads of green buckets for collecting maple syrup were hanging faithfully at their posts. How odd that these important buckets have a job which mostly just involves waiting, hanging around for the next step in the process. While they look quite inactive, they are yet indispensable to the creation of a final product. Today, Sara and I would be like buckets, hanging out and waiting for God to fill us, praying together over her next steps in the process to prepare for surgery. She had already experienced so many hours of waiting and watching.

---

[9] Karen Faulkner, "Zvi Kalisher, Holocaust Survivor, Disciple of Yeshua," Kehila News Israel, April 24, 2017, https://kehilanews.com/2017/04/24/zvi-kalisher-holocaust-survivor-disciple-of-yeshua/

[10] Zvi Kalisher, "On Prayer," *Israel My Glory: A Ministry of the Friends of Israel Gospel Ministry, Inc.* 61, no. 4, June 2003, 42.

Sara liked my maple syrup bucket analogy and agreed, "This is a visual aid for prayer. We are not the ones who send sunshine to raise up the sap. The cold at night sends sap back down the trunk. The process of waiting for clear sap means we are not really in control of anything. This is God's process.

Here comes heat and trials to purify the gallons of sap. Boiled, refined, purified, all that is a time-consuming process that we would rather skip over quickly or just avoid, but this is how the result is truly powerful, and the final product is precious and sweet. So many hours of work go into one quart."

As Sara shared Grogg and sweet cream with me, Sara had to stop a moment and talk to Google to turn down the music sweeping through the cabin. "*Hey, Google!* Volume down please." (I appreciate her nice manners but does Google care if we say *please?*) I can see how this gift from her family was instantly bringing the gift of music into her home!

Sara loves music and asked me if I had seen the new faith-based movie, *I Can Only Imagine,* which made $17.1 million when it was only expected to sell between $2 million and $4 million in tickets! What message does this send? God is always in redemption mode. Sara has seen how difficult family relationships can negatively affect some of the residents. However, forgiveness and restoration can transform their lives.

In the movie, *I Can Only Imagine*, Bart had to forgive first. Holding on to anger is like swallowing poison but expecting the other person to die. You cannot reach your fullest potential when your heart is disabled by anger or unforgiveness, as one commentator agreed, "Inspired by the miracle God worked on his dad, Bart Millard went on to write the song "I Can Only Imagine." The story is evidence of grace that sustains us…"[11]

How powerful that this generation is hungry for the miracle of forgiveness. I told Sara how the topic of forgiveness came up in my class. We were reviewing the *Psychosocial Protective Factors for Disease Prevention.*[12]

---

[11] Lauren De Bellis, "I Can Only Imagine Film" Opinion, *Fox News*, March 22, 2018, http://www.foxnews.com/opinion/2018/03/22/can-only-imagine-film-it-s-time-for-anti-christian-bigots-to-stop-mocking-and-start-listening.html

[12] "Psychosocial Protective Factors for Disease Prevention," Borgess Ascension Health, 2017, https://healthcare.ascension.org

1. Relaxation: counteracts the damage of stress
2. Exercise: improves health and decreases levels of stress, anxiety and depression
3. Optimism: Optimists have fifty percent lower risk for death than their pessimistic counterparts.
4. Humor: Laughter lowers blood pressure and promotes oxygen supply
5. Forgiveness: letting go of toxic emotions and grudges benefits the immune system
6. Social support: stress may be buffered by the presence of unconditional support. Quality not quantity is the key
7. Spirituality: hope provides protection against cardiovascular damage. Regular attendance improves social support and decreases self-destructive behavior
8. Vitality: a sense of energy and enthusiasm may be restorative and regenerative (What do you look forward to?)
9. Gratitude: Journaling or paying attention to the blessings and benefits in life is an excellent antidote.
10. Altruism: volunteering has beneficial effects for individuals including positive sense of self-esteem, worthiness, as well as social interaction.
11. Pet Ownership: Owning a pet has been associated with good cardiovascular health.

Who knew that my looking forward to meeting with Sara for coffee (numbers 6,8), relaxing one-on-one every Thursday sharing Scripture (numbers 1,7), thankful to be writing her book or taking a walk around the trails at SHALOM or even petting an alpaca (numbers 11, 10, 9, 2) could check off so many boxes. We laughed together over this (number 4). As for number 3, we agreed that Scripture gives us optimism. Lamentations 3:22–23: "Because of the LORD's great love we are not consumed, for his compassions never fail. They are new every morning, great is your faithfulness."

This just leaves one topic that we try to avoid: number 5 forgiveness. As Sara and I worked today on writing the book, we prayed together, so thankful for the blessing of God's forgiveness on the Cross; we are looking forward to Palm Sunday and Easter. Her Wednesday night Bible study on the book of Mark has also become precious to her. She offered me a challenge, "Leah, do we realize that Jesus *chose* to die so we could live?

Do we really tell Jesus, *Thy Kingdom Come, THY WILL be done?*

Do we totally embrace His Will?

Chapter 18 Challenge: His name is *Yeshua, Yaweh* is our salvation. Do you know him? Open the Word of God today to John 17 and pray from the book of your heart.

After Jesus said this, he looked toward heaven and prayed: "Father, the hour has come. Glorify your Son, that your Son may glorify you. For you granted him authority over all people that he might give eternal life to all those you have given him. Now this is eternal life: that they know you, the only true God, and Jesus Christ, whom you have sent. I have brought you glory on earth by finishing the work you gave me to do. And now, Father, glorify me in your presence with the glory I had with you before the world began."

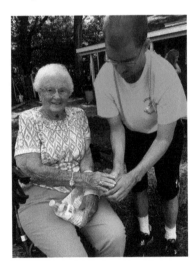

CHAPTER 19

Passed Over, Not Passed Up or Passed By!

March 29, 2018, *Maundy* Thursday. (The word *maundy* is a Latin word for *mandate* or *command*. At the Last Supper, before Jesus went to the cross, He washed His disciples' feet and gave them a new command to love one another.) Sara and I had planned to meet in the morning today, but I was home caring for our sick granddaughter who had said to me, "Nana, I want to be a white blood cell in the body of Christ!" That body of Christ imagery from Romans 12 really depicts SHALOM. The body of Christ needs every member; thus, the finger cannot say to the hand *I can get along just fine without you!* No one is passed up or passed by! Sara found her other question enlightening too, "Nana, when you say antioxidants *fight* germs, do you mean *fight* like a wrestling match where they get up or *fight* like a sword fight where someone does not get back up?"

After wrestling with the news of cancer and her upcoming surgery, Sara told me that she had a precious time of prayer this morning where *shalom*, God's peace, poured all over her. "Leah, I was so peaceful and restful that I was ready to stay here or go meet Jesus, either way. It no longer mattered."

Tonight, Sara was going to the Maundy Thursday service but also to a Good Friday service with her family to celebrate this Easter victory over death. She told me that Pastor Keith Lohman's last Sunday sermon on Isaiah 53 was visually intense. He often uses word pictures/props as he teaches residents at SHALOM. Well, he brought a huge prop to the Palm Sunday sermon! Every time he made a point from Isaiah 53, he knelt beside a large wood crossbeam on the stage. He took up a heavy hammer to pound in nails for his sermon points: Jesus was *pierced, crushed, punished* for us. The punishment that brought us *shalom* was upon Him.

Sara continued to tell me about her prayers, "Leah, I prayed '*Lord, you made this very clear that the stripes, the bleeding wounds on your back made of natural flesh, had to take my judgment for sin. This atoned for me.*' You see His beating came first. And then, there is the crown of thorns—thorns speak of the curse of sin from the book of Genesis. Jesus took on the whole curse of the ground. *Why stripes?* I asked again. *Why destroy the human flesh?* He carried the suffering and scourging as our scapegoat, as our Passover [Paschal] lamb, which is the source of my healing."

What powerful images she was thinking about. Isaiah 53 also details, "All we like sheep have gone astray." Pastor Keith certainly understands all about stray sheep after caring for the flock at SHALOM. Sheep have mob instincts and are mass-minded. If one runs, they all run astray. Timid and fearful, they also will not rest if they are scared, hungry, or bothered by pests. They don't just crave *shalom* (peace), they require it to survive.

When my young niece Holly raised a lamb for the county fair, she washed her lamb in Woolite and won a blue ribbon! A little lamb gets scared if it looks down and sees its feet. You have to hold up its head, so it looks only at you [as the shepherd], then the lamb will walk forward!

I also learned that sheep don't fight back in self-defense like other animals, so they require twenty-four-hour protection. SHALOM residents keep constant care and a watchful eye over their sheep.

To help me better understand these Passover sheep metaphors, Sara gave me her favorite book *Jewish Holy Days: Their Prophetic and Christian Significance*. It does not seem very flattering at first to be compared to sheep, as they seem very inept, often freezing in panic and acting quite dumb. However, I learned that all this imagery employs a spiritual comparison, not an intellectual one. We are spiritually helpless to save ourselves, yet we live pridefully butting one another like sheep to fight over *grass* (our wants and desires) even *bad grass*.

I knew that the lamb was worshipped in ancient Egyptian culture, so sacrificing a lamb was another act of defiance toward Egyptian authority. (The self-existent god Khnum had the head of a ram and *the first egg,* referred to as the fountain of all other creation.)

Israel's festive symbols were established by God. Jewish Scholar Coulson Shepherd writes with conviction, "No other nation ever had God establish their holidays [holy days] as Israel did while waiting supernaturally sustained in the wilderness."[1]

Coulson Shepherd outlines, "The word *feast* in Hebrew means *to keep an appointment.* God had established in Leviticus 23 The Feast of Passover and Unleavened Bread, [which point to Christ's death and burial] The Feast of Firstfruits, [Resurrection, 1 Corinthians 15:20 "But now Christ has been raised from the dead, the first fruits of those who are asleep."] Pentecost, [50 days later to establish His church with the coming of the Holy Spirit] the Feast of Trumpets [the Rapture of the Church and the regathering of Israel], Day of Atonement [*Yom Kippur:* the Time of Jacob's Trouble] and the Feast of Tabernacles [the Ultimate Salvation in the Kingdom Age of the Millennium.]"[2]

Having grown up in the synagogue, I could see now how reading the New Testament plus the Old Testament Scriptures gave Sara perspective, "the new is in the old contained; the old is by the new explained."[3]

Sara discussed with me how the Jews wanted to crucify Jesus after Passover to prevent a riot.

However, Jesus was about to fulfill the ancient feast of Passover that was required by God for the nation of Israel. Coulson Shepherd's book had offered Sara this epiphany: rabbis of old taught that the true Messiah was most likely to come on the night of Passover. I guess it is no coincidence that Sara felt so stunned by this point. She said that the Jews had wanted to crucify Jesus after the Passover, but God had already planned the date because Jesus is the Passover lamb. He could not be killed after.

He had to eat the Passover Seder with his disciples before his arrest in order to usher in the new covenant in His blood. Luke 2:20 says, "In

---

[1]   Coulson Shepherd, *Jewish holy Days: Their Prophetic and Christian Significance,* A nonprofit organization dedicated to the Lord's work and the spread of His truth (New York: Loizeaux Brothers, 1961),7.

[2]   Ibid.

[3]   Ibid.

the same way, after the supper, he took the cup saying, 'This is the new covenant in my blood, which is poured out for you.'"

In the historical book of Exodus, chapter 12, God gave instructions on the blood sacrifice for Israel's protection from the death angel. This angel was to pass over Israel before their exodus from slavery in Egypt. Their home would be saved only if they had lamb (or goat) blood placed on their doorposts. This was a picture of what Jesus was to accomplish on the cross. His sacrifice ended the covenant of 613 Jewish laws that included the Ten Commandments, which we could never perfectly keep, thus resulting in judgment. The required blood sacrifice of animals was now being replaced. Jesus established a new covenant in His own blood by covering the life of the individual believer. This new covenant must be received by faith in the finished work on the cross by the Lamb of God. For believers, God's wrath and judgment are now removed. His law is now written in their hearts. John 1:17 explains how the law was given by Moses, but this grace and truth came through Jesus Christ.

Sara was also rather excited when I told her that back in the early 1970s, I had once attended a Seder with roasted lamb, bitter herbs, and unleavened bread. The lamb shank represents *zeroa*, the sacrifice or Paschal lamb. The bitter herbs (often horseradish on romaine leaves) represent Israel's bitter servitude to Egypt. The bread without yeast, unleavened bread (matzah), was baked in a hurry since they had to leave quickly in the morning (the great Exodus) and later cross the ancient *Reed Sea; Yam Suph* in Hebrew, means the sea of reeds.

As I recall, my church did not use the modern Passover additions of salt water for their tears shed as slaves, the four cups of wine, the empty chair for Elijah, or the candles and a boiled/roasted egg to symbolize tabernacle sacrifices, or the greens and grated apple to represent the bricks which Israelites made under cruel whips as slaves in Egypt.

Like the first journey, modern-day Passovers last seven days. Amazingly, the Jewish missionaries Vernon and Faith Shannon, supported by our Decatur Bible Church, brought us that new Seder experience one Easter day! Yes, the same couple who prayed with the newly engaged Glen and Sara back in the early 1960s! Like a golden thread woven into the loom of time, we would all one day be part of the pattern of SHALOM, like kingdom art!

Of course, I did begin to see that our Seder experience in church was not like a Seder meal in Sara's family. Like families, no two Seder meals are said to be alike. Fathers begin the Seder meal by asking children "Why is this night different from all other nights?" Then the sky is the limit for how they use songs, storytelling (from the Haggadah, book/script), foods, and even pageants with costumes! Some dance over water on the floor or over water in a bucket to represent the Red Sea crossing. No one is a passive consumer.

Preparation for Passover involves an extreme ritual of house cleaning which sounds like a prep for a hospital surgical team: using boiling water and hot flames to sterilize for all fermentation. Families use new Seder dishes/utensils but also remove everything fermented (chametz) from bread to beer, plus selling or giving chametz to Gentiles, ridding the home of things like wheat, spelt, rye, and oats. Since *the house of bondage* is also said to be within, the goal of this holy day is to refresh, renew, purify, transform, cleanse.

Sara told me that Passover and Easter Day are so precious to her and are her favorite *holy days* (from where we get the word holidays).

She relates, "Leah, just as the lamb's blood in the story of the Passover had to be placed on the door frames in order for the death angel to *Pass Over* Israel and not take the first born, now the blood of Christ [the Passover Lamb] is on me and death cannot have my soul. My life is his dwelling place. I am covered by Jesus's blood. I am on sacred ground."

Being "Passed Over" is not the same as today's feeling of missing out on a facebook event or viral video on social media: *FOMO* (Fear of missing out!)[4] Fear of being *passed up or passed by* actually enslaves some users in the Facebook community. Being *Passed-over*, on the other hand, refers to the Hebrews slaves who were liberated from cruel servitude. All who put the lamb's blood on the sides and top of the door frame to their house, in a step of faith were rescued (passed over) by the death angel who took all the firstborn sons.[5] Why firstborn sons?

---

4 For more on this phenomena, see https://www.washingtonpost.com/national/health-science/research-finds-link-between-social-media-and-the-fear-of-missing-out/2013/07/08/b2cc7ddc-e287-11e2-a11e-c2ea876a8f30_story.html?noredirect=on&utm_term=.72e8e520f6a7

5 For more commentary see https://www.biblegateway.com/resources/commentaries/Matthew-Henry/Exod/Death-First-Born-Egyptians

Coulson Shepherd offers this explanation. Over three thousand years ago, Rameses II wrote, "Israel is annihilated. Israel will have no posterity!"[6]

Since Pharaoh had murdered Jewish babies in his effort to wipe out their lineage forever, God sent the tenth plague in response to a tyrant's genocide.

Yet Moses went boldly to Pharaoh, waiting through nine plagues, pleading for him to *let God's people go.* At first Moses was not so sure God had picked the right leader to challenge Pharaoh. However, this *shy guy* gained the courage to lead after God simply asked him *"What is in your hand?"* Exodus 4. Re: a shepherd's staff.

I can see now why Glen Collison *loved* this verse. God had picked this gentle man out of the flock to lead his special sheep to independence and freedom. Passover is called the *Festival of Freedom.*

The residents of SHALOM freely have regular Bible memorization and prayers together before their work days at the SHALOM Woolery. I can see how the visual lesson on sheep, goats, and lambs helps them understand these concepts! The coaches and case workers are watching residents mature, living into their fullest potential. This was always Glen's vision, to teach natural life lessons from a farm.

Coulson Shepherd writes, "When we, Jews and Gentiles, believe in Him, when we believe in our hearts that *Yeshua* is the Jewish Messiah and the world's Savior, and that He died for our sins and rose again according to the Scriptures, then we too can say as Job did [19:25–26] I know that my Redeemer liveth, and that He shall stand at the latter day upon the earth."[7]

I can see why Sara loves this small book with a star of David on the cover. The text teaches, "Without the Lamb of God now, there can be no true Passover, no deliverance. *Yeshua Hamashiach* [Jesus, Messiah] is the Lamb of God [and the Lion of Judah who fights back for his sheep.]"[8]

We stand amazed by the truth that God would reveal this, affirming we are not to be "swindled or smuggled" into the kingdom, as Shepherd explains.[9] He wants our hearts by our choice. We are chosen, yet we choose—a mystery!

---

6   Shepherd, 19.
7   Shepherd, 36.
8   Shepherd, 29.
9   Shepherd, 20.

With this sacrifice of the true Passover Lamb, we now have a new relationship of *shalom* with God and now *shalom* with one another. A Jew and an Arab can find love, friendship, and true unity in Jesus! Walls are broken down.

Passover embraces the Hebrew term *communitas,* which means that all are equal in this community of celebration/fellowship, united in liberation. Glen and Sara certainly carried this beautiful family *communitas* with them to the Homestead, and later to their nonprofit organization, SHALOM Inc.

I experienced that feeling of *communitas* on April 1, 2018, Easter Sunday! I was in church with my family, playing one of my favorite Easter hymns on the piano "Because He Lives I Can Face Tomorrow!" Pastor Keith and his dear wife Andie (a valuable partner in the SHALOM ministry) came up to the front after the service to meet my family. Sara Collison was rejoicing, calling Easter "the greatest day of the year!"

Sara enjoyed getting a card from my mom who is also a breast cancer survivor, getting diagnosed around the same age. Sara was so grateful for *communitas*, expressed by the many calls, cards, and prayers from the SHALOM Network and Haven Church and our surrounding community! I can see how she is part of a large loving family, with children and grandchildren.

Sara asked, "Leah, are you free to meet next week on your spring break? Janet and JD VanderMeer are coming from Middlebury, Indiana!" A tub of scrapbook photo albums later, I would learn how this special couple had taken the *communitas* model for SHALOM on the road, for the whole world to see and experience His love!

Chapter 19 Challenge: Jesus's name is *Yeshua HaMashiach* (Annointed, messiah)

In light of the historical context of Passover, how can you now experience a deeper meaning when you celebrate the Lord's Supper? Acts 4:12, "Neither is there salvation in any other, for there is no other name under Heaven given among men, whereby we must be saved." The name itself embodies a sacred mystery. YHVH.[10] "According to the rabbis, the first letter, yod, symbolizes humility because it is the smallest of all letters. The second letter, shin, stands high among the sacred letters because it represents two names for God, Almighty *El Shaddai* and peace, *shalom*. The third letter is vav. It represents redemption [Passover Imagery] through anguish. And the fourth letter is ayin. It symbolizes a spring of water... Yod speaks of Jesus incarnation. 'Being found in fashion as a man, he humbled himself and became obedient unto death, even death of the cross' [Philippians 2:8] Shin is found in Isaiah 9:6, His name shall be called Wonderful, Counselor, the Mighty God, the Everlasting Father, Prince of Peace. Ephesians 2:14 shows the Passover lamb, 'For Christ himself has brought peace to us. He united Jews and Gentiles into one people when, in his own body on the cross, he broke down the wall of hostility that separated us.'" John 4:14 proves he is Living Water [ayin] "but whoever drinks of the water that I will give him shall never thirst, but the water that I will give him will become in him a well of water springing up to eternal life.

Coulson Shepherd urges, "We beseech you to look away from days and observances and behold God's Lamb, Christ our Passover Lamb Sacrificed for us [1 Corinthians 5:7]."[11]

Spend some time today with someone who feels passed by or who has been passed up. Share with them the good news about being Passed Over by the blood of Jesus, the Passover Lamb!

That Christ hath regarded my helpless estate,
And hath shed His own blood for my soul.
My sin—oh, the bliss of this glorious thought!—
My sin, not in part but the whole,
Is nailed to the cross, and I bear it no more,
Praise the Lord, praise the Lord, O my soul!
For me, be it Christ, be it Christ hence to live:
If Jordan above me shall roll,
No pang shall be mine, for in death as in life
Thou wilt whisper Thy peace [*Shalom*] to my soul.[12]

---

[10] Peter Colon, "The Sweetest Name I Know," *Israel My Glory: A Ministry of the Friends of Israel Gospel Ministry, Inc.* 61, no. 4 (June 2003): 19–20

[11] Shepherd, 7.

[12] Phillip P. Bliss and Horatio B. Spafford, "It Is Well With My Soul," Words, 1873. Music, 1876.

CHAPTER 20

Taking SHALOM Inc. on the Road!

April 4, 2018. Spring break at 6191 North Riverview Drive, Kalamazoo, Michigan. Today, I drove up to Sara's cabin to meet Janet and JD VanderMeer from Encouragement Tours and Events. Their company theme is "We all need encouragement," rooted in 1 Thessalonians 5:11: "Therefore encourage one another and build each other up, just as in fact you are doing" (NIV). Encouragement is a double blessing. JD and Janet note, "We found over the years that we were often encouraged by the SHALOM residents and travelers. It was a gift of encouragement that God gave back to us—what a blessing!"

Throwing dinner rolls in a café on vacation? Yes, SHALOM residents and chaperones enjoyed that adventure in Ozark, Missouri! They liked the Lambert Café's motto: "We hope you come hungry, leave full, and hopefully have a laugh or two!"[1]

I would soon hear laughter and reminiscing over everything from throwing dinner rolls to recording an Elvis song in Studio B! These good friends of Glen and Sara and the SHALOM residents had just driven up

---

[1] Lambert's Café since 1942, https://throwedrolls.com/

to Michigan on some black icy roads from Middlebury, Indiana. They are not just *fair-weather* friends!

Sara had told me earlier, "This couple is like family, real kindred spirits on the road! I can't wait for you to meet them!"

Indeed, they were hugging and crying like old friends. JD had been at Glen's bedside in the U of M hospital, January 14, 2012, very providentially since he was driving the motor coach for a sports team and had arrived in the same city when he first got the news of Glen being admitted. He went to the University of Michigan (U of M) hospital to join that sacred circle of prayer around Sara and Glen, walking with them in those final hours. Our group shared tears of joy remembering Glen today.

JD's wife Janet had come well-prepared today to share more stories, since she had brought a gigantic heavy tub full of a dozen photo albums of their trips.

Janet explained, "We had already launched Encouragement Tours and Events for leisure when we offered business tours through another division."[2]

JD had been in management with a couple of heavy truck manufacturers and had always enjoyed getting behind the wheel, even with a suit and tie on. Their tour company has done tours nationwide but also has done tours for regional events like *Gaither Homecoming* and *Promise Keepers.*

Sara welcomed them like she had just been with them yesterday, and they picked up right where they left off. Seventeen trips can bond people like that. However, these SHALOM trips were more than just a week of entertainment.

At the time Glen and Sara discovered their services, Janet was still working full time at a Credit Union.

"Well," Janet admitted smiling. "First of all, I have to say that we had never put a package tour together before for adults with special needs/accommodations to travel like this. JD and I do not just buy into prepackaged destination trips like some tour companies. We always scouted out our destinations and events trying to eliminate negative surprises and loose ends. These trips were designed to match the client's needs, right down to the motor coach games or surprises on the road!"

I heard about the need to call ahead to secure special accommodations and the timing required to maintain medication schedules. I too

---

[2]   Encouragement Tours and Events, Division of the MTT Group, Inc., Middlebury, Indiana.

was so impressed by their tours, and by Sara and Glen's ardent pursuit to take their residents on the road. I thought, *Weren't they afraid of the massive crowds at large venues like the Grand Ole Opry or Branson, Missouri?*

Janet seemed very keen on keeping track of *her sheep*. They would grow closer on a trip as they learned to stay together and watch out for each other.

Sara reminisced, "It was such a joy to watch our residents experience new foods, see new places, do new things they had never done before. [From zip lining to wall climbing!] Glen and I were just committed to doing a yearly trip. In those early years of SHALOM [1988–1995] Glen and I did all the planning. I was still employed for the Battle Creek Veteran's Hospital [until 2009]. Yes, I was teaching CPR classes, but still working in the employee health office, giving flu shots and TB tests. Glen and I worked around that schedule to plan the trips, plus finances, organizing itinerary, maps, plans, yes, everything! [And all in an era before GPS, Google, etc.] We would find drivers, use vans, set up plans and secure chaperones, I mean our team did *everything!*"

I was impressed with the generosity of so many in the community, from donors to chaperones, who made all this possible. Our travelers often stayed at churches overnight to keep costs down. Packing sack lunches brought down meal prices too for these four to five day trips. Chaperones, caregivers and family members, plus residents with family members were all involved in the production! I could not imagine the level of energy and organization that went into packing sack lunches, medications, let alone doing the trip planning.

Glen's cheerful face is everywhere in Janet's book with detailed designs on scrapbook pages. Sara, however, confessed, "Glen often felt more like that band director in the movie *Mr. Holland's Opus*. He just kept plugging away at daily tasks, trying to do whatever was in his hand in so many creative directions, never really knowing his extraordinary level of influence on others! He still had unfinished ideas and plans for the farm. His dreams are now coming true in 2018! Glen did not know it then, but he had been called to plant *seeds*. 2 Corinthians 9:11. This most generous God who gives seed to the farmer that becomes bread for your meals is more than extravagant with you. He gives you something you can then give away, which grows into full-formed lives, robust in God, wealthy in every way, so that you can be generous in every way, producing with us great praise to God."

Just about the time that Sara and Glen were getting exhausted and running out of steam for planning trips, they met Janet and JD, a blessing from God. They were referred by an outside company.

Janet said, "Sara had asked me if we were free this one week to do a tour for them. I went to work that day at the Credit Union thinking, *I am never going to get a week off, not this very same week.* So I prayed [like those dangerous prayers that Sara prays] *Lord I will go on this trip if I get time off, which is hard to do.*"

The impossible came true, and the rest is history as they say. Janet's creatively sharp talents seem well-matched with JD's spiritual leadership/driving talents! This well-traveled pair would soon create seventeen unforgettable trips for SHALOM (1996–2013, according to the memory albums present in her tub.)

Janet's albums included detailed notes which left Sara bubbling with happiness to see them again. She explained, "We saw waitresses cry on these trips. Our residents would hug the crew and openly thank waitresses, waiters, anyone serving them. Wherever they went, they were ambassadors of *shalom,* God's peace. Hosts always said to please come back again, they enjoyed us so much."

JD also expressed the same sentiment but added, "There is a strong need to see adults with developmental disabilities interfacing with the community like this, for others out there to see our loving group together, functioning like a family, in this positive light. It is so *vital!*"

Janet concurred that she and JD had worked to orchestrate these trips with that vision in mind. They would design each trip to be educational yet interesting and inviting.

JD continued, "People often seemed jealous of our joy. We had such positive comments on the road too. People were watching us."

JD shared in the devotions, prayers, or songs too, in addition to driving. Janet would plan the whole trip with a theme name too. (My favorite theme was the SHALOM Hillbillies take Tennessee!)

A note on 2009 Nashville Memories: "Pastor Keith's devotions today reminded us of God's welcome to us and how we can welcome people we meet. Welcome and be welcomed. That is the theme today. The travelers did a great job of welcoming people throughout this week. On the coach, one side of the aisle was called the pickers, and the other side was the grinners. We take turns getting off the coach and competing in games. Aquarium restaurant has a 200,000-gallon salt water tank fish, with 1000 species, including tropical fish and sharks! As we ate, we enjoyed watching a diver feeding the fish and waving to us. Pastor Keith and Andie's daughter, Briana, joined us for dinner. [She lives in this state!] Next day we heard: know and be known, love and be loved—our theme for the day. We saw downtown Nashville, historic VictorRCA Studio B where Elvis recorded over 200 songs. The SHALOM travelers are now the Encouragement Tour Singers as we recorded an Elvis hit song, 'Can't Help Falling in Love with You!' After a busy day of being famous, and learning to line dance, we said good night to John boy and Big Boy's! Janet sure made traveling fun. We got to ride the flatboat on the enclosed river, which circles the Delta where we ate breakfast. [OpryLand Resort] There are several types of fish and the river was made out of water from all fifty states and several countries, 1700 locations in all!"

At this point, Sara poured up more tea and her famous Grogg coffee and offered Easter cookies, a traditional memory from Glen's side of the family. They had coconut green frosting on a sugar cookie bed with three jelly beans. Sara said, as a kid, Glen loved waking up on Easter morning to see the white linen table cloth spread with the memorable sweet treat from his mom, Ruth.

Sara packed a cookie for our little granddaughter waiting for me at home on spring break. My phone interrupted our meeting too, making JD smile at the informal style for an interview for the book—coffee, laughter, stories, photos everywhere, and lots of handwritten notes! Janet's phone rang next, so she stepped into Sara's "Glory Room" to hear her phone call over our laughter. Our "meeting" kept flowing with the river of memories.

Janet too had family members needing her daily care back home, a change in this couple's former busy travel schedule. SHALOM trips prepared them to lovingly step into new roles with the special needs of their young grandchildren.

Well, at this point, I had to ask: Can you share a favorite trip memory?

"Oh my, that is hard." Janet and Sara agreed almost simultaneously.

I could sure see how the residents loved it all: seeing zoos, riding through a sand dune, walking bridges, taking ferries, riding in WWII amphibious vehicles, seeing a log cabin style McDonalds and calling the taxidermy decor McAnimals! There were photo memories from Mackinac Island, Upper Michigan, to water parks and waterfalls; from the Armstrong Space & Flight Museum to the Hershey Factory, from Great Wolf Lodge, and the Creation Museum, to just sitting and laughing at Cracker Barrels, from dining at the Grand Ole Opry Resort buffets to throwing rolls, from Branson to St. Louis, and from the Wisconsin Dells to the Columbus Zoo, but remembering South Dakota brought a peal of unanimous laughter, and suddenly Sara and Janet were swaying left to right and singing, "Water, still, cool, clear water!!"

While I was missing out on the still water joke for the moment, I was not missing out on the effect on Sara. This roundtable of reunion was just what the doctor ordered. She said she needed people near her this week who could share some laughter and positive spiritual thoughts to help her not focus solely on her serious medical news. (She was already reading an oncology textbook on her own!) As the Proverbs of Solomon tells us, "A joyful heart is good medicine, but a broken spirit drains one's strength" (Proverbs 17:22).

Sara expounded, "We were at a Dude Ranch in South Dakota when a band was entertaining us at a Hoe Down. [Circle B Ranch, The Most Authentic Western Experience in Black Hills, South Dakota. Chuckwagon dinner, Western Music and panning for gold in a real Western Town.] Suddenly this old cowboy song about WATER was playing, and our group spontaneously joined in with the band, singing like a family laughing at the dinner table, just like JD was leading them to sing on the bus together. We were having so much fun in the crowded audience! We definitely livened up the place!"

JD confirmed, "We just promoted love and thankfulness together, even while others were watching."

Well, I have been to Wall Drug, South Dakota where they pass out free water, and I know how precious water is in that hot desert! That is just how Sara and Glen felt about finding JD and Janet to lead them on the road!

They all agreed that the elegant Grand Ole Opry trip really stood out. Sometimes, however, it was the little things that made such a huge difference. Instead of hearing, "Are we there yet?" like so many of us do on long vacations, they heard "What game is next?" Janet planned travel games and had prerecorded sounds or tunes to play "Name that Sound and Name that Tune!" Olympic game breaks offered them a chance to earn medals. JD kept them on schedule while Janet kept them loving the journey, from volleyball using balloons on the coach to doing Pictionary-style games.

One of their favorite games was drawing the face of someone on the motor coach then making everyone else guess who it was! SHALOM has had many great artists among the residents. Esmeralda Aguirre with MRC[3] had worked with Todd Johnson, and his amazing artwork was on display at his memorial gathering at the Shepherd's Barn back in February 2018. Todd, Jessica (and Michelle) were chosen (2016) to have their artwork displayed at Friendship Village, where it was also for sale. Other residents have won honors like that in the past too.

I was impressed with Janet's names for their trips: Rockin Arkers visited Lancaster, Pennsylvania and landed in a Kalamazoo Gazette article, "It would be hard to beat previous trips to New York, Washington, D.C.; Tennessee, Florida, Toronto, and elsewhere. But the five-day Pennsylvania trip, which included side trips to a Pretzel Factory, Harley Davidson Plant, Hershey park and countless good restaurants was definitely a hit! Sara said the group rolled dough for pretzels, sat on Harleys, got a backstage tour at the American Music Theater, and were inspired by the biblical presentation of Noah at the 2,000 seat Millennium that included a combination of real animals and mechanical ones."

Sara noted, "The costuming and the whole thing was phenomenal. You thought rain was coming down on your head[during the flood] It was so real."

---

[3] MRC artWorks—a program of MRC Industries, Inc.—provides adults living with developmental disabilities an outlet to achieve creative self-expression in a way that promotes personal growth, dignity, and self-confidence. Located in the heart of downtown Kalamazoo.

For them, this trip is the highlight of their year. The Pennsylvania Trip comes on the heels of the 14th Anniversary of the Americans with Disabilities Act. [1990–2014]."[4]

I loved reading about all these trips. JD added seriously, "These trips expanded their world, gave them more independence too. We really watched them grow over the years. [1996–2013]. I remember one resident who barely smiled and did not talk at all on that first trip. He really came out of his quiet shell the more trips he went on with us. He just responded to this family style bond that we shared together on the road."

I could visualize that bond when I saw the photo of the Wisconsin cheesehead hat covered in everyone's signatures, and a basketball with signatures too. There was also a photo frame with the names all stitched by Sara's professional sewing machine.

As to expanding horizons, Pastor Keith apparently had played mini golf in a hotel hallway, and residents wore grass skirts and what? Coconuts? Yes, those fun moments were bonding for sure. Sara's phone rang next in the middle of our "official interview/meeting to write chapter 20." Sara had to stop and field the call since the request was for new openings at the Homestead. Ah, Growth!

I suppose that Janet and JD were not sure what to expect either when they first got involved on trips. Janet remembers her early days of coaching residents not to be afraid of the large staircase getting off the motor coach. They just built trust over the years. In 2008, Kathy Lesman wrote about one trip:

We pulled into the Homestead driveway [Kalamazoo] at 6:30 a.m. to load up on JDs Motor Coach—all

---

[4]   Dave Person, "Road Trip," City Life, *Kalamazoo Gazette*, June 25, 2004, 3.

fifty-four seats are full! Pastor Keith's devotion was on 'Who is God the Creator?' It was easy to see the truth as we saw the sun come up on our beautiful surroundings. After games on the motor coach we arrived at Holiday Inn in Lexington, Kentucky, our home for the next four nights. Day 2: Devotions today offered another question for us: Who is Jesus? Which brought a good response from travelers: Our Savior if we are following Him. Lunch at the Cracker Barrel then on to Kentucky Horse Park, a 2,000-acre park! We got to see buildings being built in preparation for the 2010 World Equestrian Games (first time outside of Europe) and one-half mile race track!

In addition to reading these interesting notes, we kept looking at photos and postcards. John 13:35 came to mind, "By this shall all men know you are my disciples by how you love one another." The bond on trips was evident. "Forty-four travelers and chaperones had a memorable time in Frankenmuth, September 5–7, 2014. We traveled in four vans and stayed at Covenant Hills Camp. At the camp we enjoyed a horse and wagon ride, many gym and game activities, and the now famous zip line over the lake! Old cars cruised the streets of Frankenmuth. Grandpa Tiny's Farm had many animals willing to be petted and loved. While there we were given the surprise of our first Nigerian Dwarf goat, a buck, which we call Papa Tiny, now residing at the SHALOM Farm! The Zeilinger Wool Company hosted a tour that really intrigued all involved in our SHALOM Woolery! The chicken dinner at Zehender's and shopping at Bronner's were special treats! After a meaningful time of worship, we headed home, stopping for a game of miniature golf in Battle Creek and dinner at Culvers! It was an amazing adventure!"

Before we left Sara's cabin that afternoon, JD led us in prayer for SHALOM, and for Keith, and for Sara's upcoming surgery for cancer. Then we were all on the road again, ready to show *shalom* to a hungry world!

April 10, 2018. Tuesday at 6191 North Riverview Drive, Kalamazoo, Michigan.

Today my granddaughter and I went to the SHALOM farm to visit Sara before surgery. Sara's friends Janet, Jeannie, Dee, and family members, were going to be with Sara during her surgery. Outside in the yard, our granddaughter greeted SHALOM residents Calvin, Diane, and Angie who were taking a cool evening walk and checking for any signs of Spring. They introduced her to Moses the orange cat!

We would not know until tomorrow evening how God would answer all our serious prayers for Sara and Pastor Keith. Today we were just walking around and waiting, encouraging our hearts together. So many were praying! I had chosen to pray through the Passover Hallel, sung by Jesus and His Disciples at the Last Supper, Psalms 113 to 118. Would surgery be like a Red Sea crossing where a solid path of deliverance was planned, even though they were so afraid at first to cross over? Psalm 118 is exceptionally joyous where we always dance with joy for earthly and yet eternal *shalom.*

The residents laughed when we arrived and our granddaughter greeted them, "Hello I am the next generation!" (We told her that a *family tree* is not a literal tree.) They took her to the barn to see the newborn goats. She was mesmerized by it all. Samuel the rambunctious alpaca looked like he was getting ready for his next "haircut" to make more dryer balls. The *new friends,* as she called the residents, taught her to stay calm around him and not to run or panic, and not to be afraid. She asked them, "Is this your house? Do you own it?" She did not understand the term AFC (Adult Foster Care). The concept of a family style *forever home,* however, offers so much support yet freedom. I was seeing Glen's goal of "sustainability" in action.

Before we left, we said goodbye to the baby goat "kids"! I was thinking about how my Aunt Maggie was rescued by goat's milk. She was born in March, at home on the muck farm, over eighty years ago, weighing only two-point-five pounds but breathing on her own! Her family kept her skin hydrated by rubbing it with olive oil. My Dutch grandfather fed her goat's milk with a small dropper, keeping her warm in a basket with a warm water bottle by the old cookstove. With two toddlers, and a recovering wife, this godly man cared for them all at home around the clock! He also gave my auntie a Dutch nickname which means miracle baby. By God's miracle design, she would grow stronger to one day work in the baby medical records department![5] When Aunt Maggie met Sara, I smiled thinking that one was saved by a lamb (wool coat) and one was saved by a goat! Both are saved by Jesus, so the bond lasts to eternity.

---

5   Lakeland Regional Healthcare, Saint Joe, MI: "Service Awards 2011, Maggie Waterlander 55 years of service," YouTube, https://www.youtube.com/watch?v=bQKWYdFBY5A

One more young heart joined the kingdom since the writing of this book. September 14, 2017, our granddaughter and I had a long chat at bedtime. She was suddenly worried about the *forever* stuff. We read John 3:16 "For God so loved the world that he gave his only begotten son, that whoever believes on him will not perish but have everlasting life." She prayed a simple prayer: "Dear God, *this* sounds wonderful. Good night."

Another journey toward *shalom* has begun.

Chapter 20 Hebrew Challenge: His name is *Yeshua Hamashiach,* Jesus our Annointed Messiah. Do you know Him? Do you share Him with others?

John 8:58 Jesus said unto them, "Truly, I say to you, before Abraham was, I am."

The name Jesus is an English transliteration of the Greek, IESOUS, a supremely sovereign name of the true and living God. The miracles Jesus did on earth and the prophecies fulfilled speak to the power of His name. *Yeshua* involves the Hebrew verb for saves, helps, the Lord is our Deliverance.[6]

John 4:25, The woman [at the well who had been with five husbands and was living with another man] said to Him, "I know that Messiah is coming [He who is called Christ], when that One comes, He will declare all things to us." Jesus said to her, "I who speak to you am *He.*"

---

6   Peter Colon, "The Sweetest Name I Know," *Israel My Glory, Friends of Israel,* July/August 2003, 61, no. 4, 20.

What is in Your Hand?

By Rev. Keith Lohman,
excecutive director of SHALOM Inc.

F ifth grade, Hamilton, Michigan. We just left him there. The bell rang to come in for class, and we just left him, stuck in the slushy snow we had formed into a sort of "dare you" bridge to cross the small creek. Kevin, the class tease, thick glasses, crooked teeth, intellectual disability, was stuck in the slush, shin deep. I walked away laughing with the others and wondered how Kevin would get out. He did, but not to my credit.

Why do I remember that? Because I still see Kevin stuck. Yelling for help. I hear him. I wish I could go back there with who I am now and be his advocate, his friend.

Sixth grade, another guy. My teacher, Mrs. Dieters, called me aside. "Could you help Steve with this lesson, please? You seem to be the only one to be friends with him." Steve was also a class tease, a bit slow, awkward. I was told I was his friend.

Why do I remember that? Because my identity was now "friend and helper." I had become an ally of my peers who live with disabilities. An advocate. A partner.

Now fifty years later I have the best job I could imagine. I work with the incredible people of SHALOM and our growing numbers of community friends and families living with disabilities. *I believe with all my heart that God knew I would need this kind of place—to teach me what He wants me to know of Him.* He is known through Kevin and Steve and how He loves me through them and loves them through me.

I have learned so many things here at SHALOM. Take this as your challenge to learn what God is teaching you wherever you are. Please do not miss the lessons God is teaching you this week. Ask Him to show you. Here are some things God has put in my hand, and in my heart.

1. *I am very performance-oriented.* But I cannot perform myself to God. My value is in God's performance. Someday I will no longer be able to perform my duties. There is a time coming when I will not be able to think clearly, move freely, catch my balance. I will not be able to feed myself or control my bladder. Each day brings me closer to my own disabilities in my own eyes and before God. What will I be when I am disabled? Does my identity change? Am I less valuable then? Am I a problem to be solved? *I want to know I will be valued even when I am not able to perform.*

Jesus already did everything. It's His performance, not mine, that saves me and equips me to serve. So when I am with people who are living with disabilities, God helps me see Him and what He has done. He shows me value apart from performance. He teaches me to recognize value apart from performance. Ephesians 2:8–10, "For it is by grace you have been saved, through faith—and this is not from yourselves, it is the gift of God—not by works, so that no one can boast. For we are God's handiwork, created in Christ Jesus to do good works, which God prepared in advance for us to do."

2. *My call is to walk with broken people toward wholeness in Christ.* This means I need to slow down my pace to match the one with whom I walk or stop pretending that I care. "My command is this: Love one another as I have first loved you" John 15:12. *We are all broken people finding our wholeness in Jesus.*

3. My weakness is an opportunity for God's strength. So is someone else's weakness. My weakness is not more important than yours.

This being true, I had better learn to leave opportunity for God to work in me through the inadequacies of others and to *bless* me through their weakness. 2 Corinthians 12:9–10, But he said to me, "My grace is sufficient for you, for my power is made perfect in weakness. Therefore I will boast all the more gladly about my weaknesses, so that Christ's power may rest on me. That is why, for Christ's sake, I delight in weaknesses, in insults, in hardships, in persecutions, in difficulties. For when I am weak, then I am strong."

4. The ability to see God's Glory is not performance based. Seeing God's Glory is, at its heart, submission based. Those with a disability of the heart do not submit, nor do they see God's glory.

God's glory is visible only by submission. If I have not seen His glory recently, it is not His fault.

I need to check my submission level and my heart. People who live with disabilities are often the first to point out God's beauty, His compassion, forgiveness and mercy. They get it because their heart is submitted. What is the status of my heart?

Exodus 33:18–19, Then Moses said, "Now show me your glory." And the LORD said, "I will cause all my goodness to pass in front of you, and I will proclaim my name, the LORD, in your presence. I will have mercy on whom I will have mercy, and I will have compassion on whom I will have compassion."

5. People often have a surprising spiritual depth under the shallowness of my first impression. Matthew 11:25–26, At that time Jesus said, "I praise you, Father, Lord of heaven and earth, because you have hidden these things from the wise and learned and revealed them to little children. Yes, Father, for this is what you were pleased to do."

6. How I looked when I had a missing front tooth a couple years ago made me feel very awkward. Why is that? When I was eight, a missing front tooth was an honor. Now I feel so awkward. I liked being eight better. Maybe that's why those living with disabilities of all kinds often seem to be about eight, while I'm stuck being fifty-nine and feeling really awkward. People with disabilities are often more comfortable in their skin than those who hide their disabilities. Acceptance is an amazing thing.

7. Be ready to see angels. If I am not seeing angels, check my hospitality toward strangers. Another heart issue. Hebrews 13:2 says "Do not forget to show hospitality to strangers, for by so doing some have shown hospitality to angels without knowing it." (Hospitality equals love toward strangers) (do not forget equals don't be neglectful) SHALOM in God's Kingdom means there are no strangers. No one is left out.

8. The call of God is not diminished by disability. And your call is not diminished by your uninformed sense of inadequacy! He calls us to His mission. Those living with disabilities are called to Kingdom Mission and tend to accept the call. I hope to someday catch up to their ability and passion to follow Christ!

9. To disciple a person living with disabilities is an effort twice blessed. First, what an honor to speak into someone's life so eager to know God wants to use them! Second, I have rarely given more than I have received.

10. Many disabilities are not by choice; but some are. And those are the worst kind. That's a disability of the heart. Some examples of disabilities of choice are grudges, unforgiveness, a dismissive attitude, condescension, pride, a low value for people, a lack of respect. There is a Healer for disabilities of the heart. His name is Jesus.

11. Disabilities have their limitations. Think about that—disabilities (which by definition are limitations)—are limited!

Disabilities cannot disable the soul, or joy, or peace, or love, or hope. They cannot limit kindness or goodness, generosity or creativity; they cannot stop dreams or determination, imagination or friendship; they cannot prevent gentleness or kindness, curiosity, humor or significance. Need me to list more? How is your life going?

12. There is a wholeness that disabilities cannot touch, the wholeness given by Jesus. Disabilities can't touch this. Our limitations do not limit God. Nor do they diminish what God is doing. Only disabilities of choice (my sin) can limit the wholeness of Jesus I experience.

13. I am responsible to be an advocate for those who cannot be for themselves. And that does not mean just waiting for an opportunity; it means taking the opportunity to make someone's life better.

14. God is pro-life. What the world would often throw away—are God's treasures. Am I treasuring those whom God treasures?

15. My highest calling is to grow up to be like a child. Therefore, I have to hang around those whom I want to be like. I am.

16. The principle of the Body of Christ DEMANDS that I learn to honor those who seem to me have the least to give. 1 Corinthians 12:22–27, "Those parts of the body that seem to be weaker are indispensable, and the parts that we think are less honorable we treat with special honor. And the parts that are unpresentable are treated with spe-

cial modesty, while our presentable parts need no special treatment. But God has put the body together, giving greater honor to the parts that lacked it, so that there should be no division in the body, but that its parts should have equal concern for each other. If one part suffers, every part suffers with it; if one part is honored, every part rejoices with it." Now you are the body of Christ, and each one of you is a part of it.

17. Both Satan and God are claiming to tell the Truth about disabilities and the people who live with them—who will I believe? Who is teaching me today? From whom do I seek my understanding? I need to hear the voice of Jesus.

18. I am in awe of people who live with disabilities all their lives, every minute, and never whine or complain about it. Instead, they befriend me, a whiner and complainer. Philippians 2:14–16, "Do everything without grumbling or arguing, so that you may become blameless and pure, children of God without fault in a warped and crooked generation. Then you will shine among them like stars in the sky as you hold firmly to the word of life."

19. The Holy Spirit does not recognize disabilities. Why should He? His job is to convince of Truth—of the power and strength and blessing of God's abilities! There is no room for dissing the abilities of God, and even small abilities given to Him to use. Nothing given to God is small. John 6:5–14, Here is a boy with five small barley loaves and two small fish, but how far will they go among so many? Jesus said, "Have the people sit down." There was plenty of grass in that place, and they sat down (about five thousand men were there). Jesus then took the loaves, gave thanks, and distributed to those who were seated as much as they wanted. He did the same with the fish. When they had all had enough to eat, he said to his disciples, "Gather the pieces that are left over. Let nothing be wasted." So they gathered them and filled twelve baskets with the pieces of the five barley loaves left over by those who had eaten.

20. My true identity is in Christ. Period. Anything else I think of myself is either trivial or a lie. That includes self-sufficiency and what I consider my greatest abilities. All trash when compared to Christ! Philippians 3:7–9, "But whatever were gains to me I now consider loss for the sake of Christ. What is more, I consider everything a loss because of the surpassing worth of knowing Christ Jesus my Lord, for whose

sake I have lost all things. I consider them garbage, that I may gain Christ and be found in him, not having a righteousness of my own that comes from the law, but that which is through faith in Christ—the righteousness that comes from God on the basis of faith."

Same goes for the ones I serve. Their identity is in Christ. Period. Anything else I think of them is either trivial or a lie.

21. The kingdom of God BELONGS to such as these. I want to grow up to be like a child.

Mark 10:13–16 "Truly I tell you, anyone who will not receive the kingdom of God like a little child will never enter it."

22. I am often in a rush. I miss blessings because I rush by. I am too busy for flowers with broken petals. I have to get stuff done, check off my list, move quickly, stop wasting time. I try time management tricks. I keep a list. I prioritize. I work longer. I get frustrated and impatient. It shows up in my relationships as I isolate and growl and use and abuse people.

God is teaching me a new kind of being called patience. *Patience is slowing down until the person next to me feels valued.*

23. Jesus restores my dignity. If I ever doubt God's call on my life all I need do is recall a trip when the biggest guy you ever saw had an explosion of peanut butter cup diarrhea. Down both legs and onto his shoes. And I had the privilege of cleaning him up in folds of fat from his waist to his feet. I cannot think of anything that should be more disgusting, more humiliating, to him and to me. He thanked me and tried to pay me cash. I got to turn that down and look him in his eyes and call him my brother in Christ and told him I love him.

Jesus loves me like that. He loves you like that. He restores your dignity. He turns down your offer to pay Him. He calls you His Sister, His Brother—and shows you how much He loves you again and again.

24. I feel great when I serve from my heart and with my heart and see a difference. Everybody can be great because anybody can serve.

Mark 10:42–45, Jesus called them together and said, "You know that those who are regarded as rulers of the Gentiles lord it over them, and their high officials exercise authority over them. Not so with you. Instead, whoever wants to become great among you must be your servant, and whoever wants to be first must be slave of all. For even the Son of Man did not come to be served, but to serve, and to give his life as a ransom for many."

Where is Kevin in your life? Is he stuck? Does he need a friend? What will you do? What is in your heart?

Are you being asked to help Steve? Are you surprised that God would entrust you with such a calling?

What is in your hand?

What calling and resources and needs are at hand right now?

How are you responding?

The most important thing about what is in your hand is not what it is, or how much you have, but your willingness to give it and submit.

And that comes from your heart. Start there. I am.

Thank you!

All proceeds from this book go to SHALOM Inc.
Thank you to all who pray!
Thank you to all who volunteer!
Thank you to all who support us by buying our book, wool products and other store/farm items.
Thank you to all who give money or donate items for our store.
Thank you to our *Jehovah Jireh.*
SHALOM Inc. depends on the financial gifts of individuals, churches and civic organizations. We are a nonprofit 501(c) (3) faith-based organization.

SHALOM board of Directors, 2018.
Phil Vlietstra, President
Sara Collison, Vice President
Garry Walton, Clerk
Rod Rieth, Treasurer
Dee Crittenden
Robin Ipema
Patricia Pinkster
Gary Steensma
Keith Lohman, Executive Director.

What is SHALOM, Inc.?

SHALOM is an acronym for Self-Help Alternative Living Opportunities of Michigan. We are a nonprofit, independent, 501 (c) (3) corporation with a Board of Directors providing oversight. SHALOM exists to serve adults living with developmental disabilities.

We are people focused, Christ-centered and community supported. The Shepherd's Barn, Connection Depot Thrift Store, The SHALOM Woolery and Farm are means to serve those whom we have been called to love.

Our desire is to reach all people with the love and wholeness we ourselves are receiving through Christ.

We have always worked with *what is in our hand.* The right people and resources always seem to be there at just the right time. Only God could do this great thing!

We welcome volunteers.

Contact us at
SHALOM Inc. Kalamazoo
6276 N. Riverview Drive
(mail to: PO Box 265)
Kalamazoo, Michigan, 49004
Contact the SHALOM office at shalomkazoo@aol.com
or call 269-382-3840.

Serving adults with disabilities through the love and wholeness of Jesus Christ:

Dear Keith Lohman, first, please convey our congratulations to Sara Collison and her friend Leah Wendt on the upcoming publication of their book. It is truly a great achievement, and we look forward to reading it. I was thinking back to the very early days when I sat in on meetings that my dad (Richard Swiat) had with Tom Hill about SHALOM and their mission. What a great story SHALOM has written and what an affirmation of the power of faith. I know my father recognized the great potential of SHALOM many years ago, and the Foundation he and my mother created is specifically designed to assist organizations such as SHALOM. It has been our mission to carry out my folk's vision for the Foundation, and SHALOM and your success and careful stewardship has reassured us that we are faithfully carrying out the wishes my folks intended when they created the Foundation. Generally, we prefer no special recognition when awarding grants because we feel we are mainly carrying out the idea conceived by our parents. However, SHALOM is a special case which truly represents why the Foundation was created. We would be honored if our mother and dad, Richard J and Frances B Swiat were mentioned in Sara's book as we feel SHALOM epitomizes their goal in creating the Richard J and Frances B Swiat Foundation. Thank you for your incredible leadership and thank you to all the people who have worked so hard to make SHALOM the success it is today. We are also very inspired and thankful for the power of God. Our thanks to everyone at SHALOM Inc. for thinking of us. Rick & Shelly Swiat

As a Board Certified Psychiatric-Mental Health Registered Nurse, Licensed Nursing Home Administrator, Sara Collison worked in a congregate facility, and as Adjunct Faculty for Kellogg Community College teaching CPR. Sara graduated from Bronson Methodist School of Nursing in Kalamazoo, Michigan in 1965, then married Glen Collison (1965) to serve the Lord together and raise their three children. She was given the 1993 Secretary's Award from the Battle Creek Veteran's Administration for Nursing Excellence with a hospital-wide impact.

In 1990, Sara and her husband Glen Collison (1941-2012) started a 501(c) (3) non-profit organization called SHA-LOM Inc. (an acronym for Self Help Alternative Living Opportunities of Michigan) which provides housing, educational, recreational and work opportunities for adults with develop-mental disabilities. Sara continues to serve as Vice President on the SHALOM Board of Directors, living in Kalamazoo, Michigan.

While Sara Collison grew up in a Jewish home, coauthor Leah grew up in an Arab-Dutch home.

Leah Wendt graduated with her Bachelor of Arts in English Literature from Grand Rapids (Michigan) Baptist College (1982) and her Master of Arts in English Literature from Western Michigan University in Kalamazoo, Michigan (1983) keeping a private piano studio since

1985. As Adjunct Faculty for Cornerstone University's Professional & Graduate Studies (PGS), she has taught English Literature, Fine Arts, and Research/ Writing courses for both onground and online classrooms. In 2016, Leah was awarded the PGS Colleen Smith Teaching in Excellence Award. She and her husband Roy (married 1984) reside in Kalamazoo, Michigan, where they raised their two children.

CPSIA information can be obtained
at www.ICGtesting.com
Printed in the USA
LVHW012029080419
613326LV00027B/1146/P